DIFFERENTIATING INSTRUCTION
in a Whole-Group Setting

**Taking the Easy
FIRST STEPS
into Differentiation**

by *Patricia Pavelka*

Husky Trail Press LLC
East Lyme, CT

Husky Trail Press LLC
PO Box 705
East Lyme, CT 06333
860-739-7644
888-775-5211
860-691-8066 fax
www.huskytrailpress.com

Editor: Lois Schenking
Cover Design: Coni Porter
Illustrations: Patrick Vincent

ISBN No. 978-1-935258-02-5

Printed in the United States of America
First edition   10 9 8 7 6 5 4 3 2 1

Acknowledgements

Thank you to:

Mom for always being an inspiration in all I do.

Lois Schenking for your constant patience and diligence
as you edited this book.

Coni Porter for the cover and the window designs. They look great.

Jo-Ann Geida for all your understanding and encouragement
with anything and everything.

Patrick Vincent for all the inside book illustrations.
You are incredibly talented.

Pam Terry for all your "landscaping" advice.

Pat Terry for being my number one CAO.

The dedicated **Staff at Howard School** in Tennessee for sharing your
classrooms with me.

Gillie Ocepeck for sharing your students' writing with me.

Betty Hollas for sharing the *Differentiating Instruction* book series.

Lorraine Walker for having confidence in me.

Deb Fredericks for all your assistance.

John Geida for all your ideas and suggestions. You really put the icing
on the cake.

Richard LaPorta my toughest critic and biggest fan.

Contents

Introduction

You can ease your way into differentiation without giving up on the whole group setting with which many of us are very comfortable. If I think about most of my teaching, it was done in a whole group setting. In today's classrooms, we teach students who have a wide-range of abilities and experiences and who all learn at different rates. When we are working with the whole class, all of these different personalities and learning styles come together. Here lies the challenge: to meet the needs of all these students. Some students already have the answer before you finish asking the question and others still do not know the answer after they have heard it a number of times.

Differentiated instruction helps all students because it engages them in activities that better respond to their individual learning needs, strengths, and desires. Therefore as educators, we are on a journey to be more responsive to different learning needs, learning styles, and personalities. Differentiating instruction in a whole-group setting can be manageable and fun; and it can bring excitement and motivation to students' learning.

"Good differentiation does not require throwing out all your planning from the past two, five, ten, or fifteen years. Good differentiation means examining how well you're providing variety and challenge in learning, identifying who among your students is best served by your current plans, and modifying those plans as needed so more students can be successful learners." Diane Heacox

In this book we will be looking at five Windows of Opportunity.

Student Engagement Window

Key concepts include:
- Ways to get all students actively involved in learning.
- Supporting and extending learning based on students' needs and curriculum expectations.
- Bringing movement to lessons.
- Helping students actively interact with both the content and their peers.
- Ways to get students' attention and shorten transition times.

Questioning Window

Key concepts include:
- Ways to get all students actively involved in questioning.
- Helping students to generate good, thought-provoking questions.
- Ensuring that we, as educators, ask high level questions.
- Giving students the structures they need to independently ponder and ask good, deep, meaningful questions.

Flexible Grouping Window

Key concepts include:
- Grouping students according to their needs and curriculum expectations.
- Grouping students based on various needs of support and challenges within a peer group.
- Working with combinations of whole group, small groups, quads, trios, and/or partners.

Differentiated Assignments Window

Key concepts include:
- Managing the assignment time so students are independently working without interrupting small groups meeting with you.
- Modeling which plays an integral part in how successfully and easily students complete assignments independently.
- Ensuring that students know where to go for help and what to do when work is completed.
- Activities and assignments that students can be working on while the teacher is meeting with small groups.
- Creating multi-leveled assignments so that students of different abilities may benefit from them.

Ongoing Assessment Window

Key concepts include:
- Ongoing assessments that drive our instruction and small group formations.
- Assessments taking place during whole group instruction and small group instruction
- Giving students different ways to "show what you know."
- Using anecdotal records for reading.

Each Window of Opportunity will have a preface that is written in a one-column format. Following the preface will be all of the ideas, activities and strategies. These will be written in a two-column format with a title and corresponding window. There will be one or two pages at the end of each window section to write down ideas, connections, and implementation strategies.

Differentiating instruction in your classroom does not have to be overwhelming. This book will help ease your way into differentiation using the five Windows of Opportunity. You'll see easy-to-use activities and routines that will enable you to have success with differentiation in your own classroom. It will allow students the freedom to manage their own learning and achievement. You can do it! Let's dive into differentiation and look at our five windows.

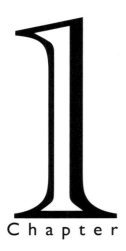

1

Chapter

Student Engagement Window

Preface

Vygotsky has "insisted that learning is social." Therefore, teachers must listen to students while teaching and peers must listen and observe to help each other learn. I must admit I did not like this research because it meant my students needed to be talking to learn. And sometimes I felt like they talked too much! However, once I took a deep breath and channeled the talking into meaningful processing, making connections and teaching each other, the talking became an integral part of the teaching. The key is: we must keep all students active and engaged during the teaching/learning process.

Getting all students actively involved in learning is often difficult, as we usually have the same five students who always read aloud, answer the questions, and yell out comments. Our goal is to ensure that all students process and understand the information being presented. We need to support those who need support, as well as challenge and extend the learning for those who are ready. We also need to bring movement, excitement, and motivation into learning. Children are always motivated for something; it's just not always what we want. We need to attract their attention and interest, which will then motivate them.

When working in a whole class setting, there is never the perfect way to impart information so they will all understand and internalize it. We must differentiate the way we work with our whole class in:

> how we give the information,
> how they process the information,
> and how they interact with one another.

Donald Graves, a colleague and friend, once said to me, "The one who does the talking does the learning." Boy, did I learn a lot in my years of teaching. We need to shift that paradigm of the teacher talking and place it on the students. The more they talk, the more they interact, the more they move, *the more they learn*. And that's what it is all about. In this student engagement window you will see a variety of multisensory activities and approaches. This is what differentiating is all about. Look at Glasser's research.

We Learn

10% of what we read
20% of what we hear
30% of what we see
50% of what we both see and hear

Do not stop here! *Keep Going*!

70% of what is discussed with others
80% of what we experience personally
95% of what we teach to someone else

Let's dig into this piece of research.

We Learn

10% of what we read
> This is when we ask students to read a selection silently.

20% of what we hear
> This is when we read to students and they are listening; or when we "teach by lecture."

30% of what we see
> This is when students are looking at visuals, maps, charts, etc. This is also when we show students pictures, diagrams, etc.

50% of what we both see & hear
> OK, so we are reading to students and they are hearing us. We are also showing students visuals, but here is the problem: their comprehension level is only at the fiftieth percentile, which is not acceptable.

Look at what happens when students just *talk* to someone…

70% of what is discussed with others
    Their achievement jumps to 70%.

80% of what we experience personally

95% of what we teach to someone else
    Their achievement jumps to 95% when they have to teach and reteach the
    information to someone else.

Notice the space and the note between 50% and 70%. The teaching is actually the 10%-50% items. And that's usually where I stopped. I gave information to my students. They read, I read, they saw visuals; so I went through the 10-50% process. That's where the teaching stopped and the processing never took place.

I'd ask students if they understood and they would all nod their heads, "Yes." I'd ask if they had any questions and no one answered, so they were sent off to work on an assignment that had to do with what was just taught. Now remember, they all said, "Yes, we understand and no, we have no questions." So why, then, within one minute of beginning their work was there:

    a line at my desk for questions?
        students roaming the room?
            students lined up at the pencil sharpener?
            arguments about the assignments?
            the list could go on.

I had forgotten or ignored the rest of this research: 70-95% is the processing. This student engagement window will help you remember and apply the processing piece to your teaching. And once the students have really processed the information, assignments and work time will go more smoothly and quietly. When students are actively engaged in the learning, talking about the information, moving and doing, applying and utilizing the information, their achievement increases.

Here is another example showing that when students are actively engaged by talking about the information, moving and doing, applying and utilizing the information; their achievement increases.

HOW WE LEARN

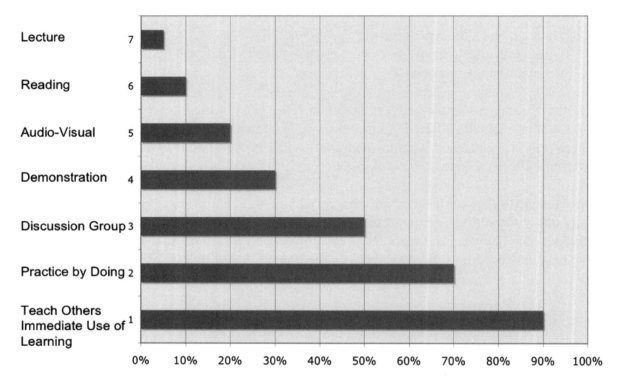

National Training Laboratories, Bethel, ME

Building relationships and getting students excited to learn is a big part of student engagement. My Goddaughter has picked out her second grade teacher for next year already. She wants Ms. LaPorta because she always smiles at her and says, "Hello." You'll also see activities in this window that build rapport between you and your students as well as your students among themselves.

Student Engagement, here we go…

Teach Using Students' Names

What a better way to get students' attention then to call their names! Almost anything can be taught and practiced using your students' names. You'll need something to write students' names on and something to put their names in. For example, write each child's name on an index card and put the cards in a container. Another idea is to write names on popsicle sticks and put them in a container.

To Support Struggling Learners: When a struggling
learner's (SL) name is pulled, another name is also pulled. The teacher now has two names. The second child must use the SL's name in an answer or example. This takes the pressure off the struggler to come up with an answer or example in front of peers. But here is the catch; after the second child gives the example or

answer, the SL must repeat what was said and, if desired, can add more information. This works, if by chance, the second name you pull is a stronger learner. But what happens if the two names you pull are both struggling learners? Then pull as many names as you need until a name comes up that is a stronger learner. You will then have possibly three or four repeaters depending upon how many names you had to pull. Do not show students the names you pull right away. I show them the sticks or cards after the activity is over. You don't want them to know the order that you pulled the names, but you do want them to know that you truly did pull those names.

For More Abled Learners:
When a proficient learner's name is pulled, you could show and say the name right away. A second name is then pulled and the proficient learner must apply and utilize the curriculum being taught to the name that was just pulled.

Let's look at different curriculum areas and how names can be used to practice and enhance learning. Students are motivated and excited to hear and use their names.

Math

Word Problems: Pull a name. Use that name in a word problem.

Kate was playing outside. Three friends came over to visit. How many were outside playing together?

Money: Pull a name. Use that name in a money situation.

Timisha went to the store with a twenty-dollar bill. She bought a book for $14.99. How much money did she have after buying the book?

Fractions: Pull four names. Those students stand together. Pull another name and that child has to put the four peers into fraction groups. Two stand here and two stand there. The twos are ½ and ½. Three stand there and one stands here. The three are ¾ and the one is ¼.

Language Arts

Contractions: Pull a name. Use that child's name in a sentence that contains a contraction.

Dana doesn't have four dogs.

Drawing Conclusions: Pull a name. Use that name in a scenario that models drawing conclusions.

Lynetta is skipping home from school. She has a big smile on her face and is swinging her arms from side to side. How does Lynetta feel? How do you know?

Letter and Sounds: Pull a name. Look at that person. Think of as many things that are associated with the letter you are working with and the child whose name was pulled.

We are working with the letter "R." Timisha has on a *red* sweater. Her socks are *red*. She has *really* nice sneakers. She had *raisins* for snack. She played with me outside at *recess*.

Colors: Pull a name. That child has to tell another student (chosen by pulling a name) to walk over to something in the classroom that is a certain color.

Kate, walk over to the yellow pencil on Ms. LaPorta's desk.

Laretha, walk over to the yellow banana that is on the food poster.

Judy, walk to the yellow jacket.

Three End Punctuation Marks:

Pull a name. Use that name in three sentences with three different punctuation marks.

Phyllis has a pretty shirt on today.
Where did Phyllis buy her shirt?
Look out, Phyllis, there's a snake behind you!

Below are Some Sample Topics for Science and Social Studies:

Urban, Suburban, and Rural
Living vs Nonliving
Magnets
Transportation
Animals
The Ocean
Land Forms
The Farm

Students' names are pulled out of the can and depending on the topic, they apply and utilize that information using the peer's name that is pulled.

You can also use index cards with words on them to add to this name activity. Pull ten names from the can and give those ten children a card. Then pull another name. That student must ask each child with a card a question. For example: "John, does your card have something on it that a magnet would attract?" "Jamal, if your card has something that a magnet would attract say, "Yes." If it does not, tell us something that a magnet would attract."

The list is endless! Anything you teach can be practiced, applied, and extended using students' names, their interests, and ideas.

Look at the My Name Your Name activity found on pages 90 and 91 for more ideas where students' names can be used.

Good Morning

Reader's Digest had an article in December, 2008 that was titled, "Hello, Everybody." The article talked about the importance of the word "hello" and what it really means.

"…saying hello is more than just saying hello. It is an acknowledgement of existence. It is a pause, however brief, to affirm another's worth…How might the world change…if we mastered this word?" The article went on to tell about a middle school that had its teachers greet students individually every morning. "This brief interaction ultimately raised the kids' productivity by 27%….it resulted in more class participation and better grades."

WOW! Just by saying the word "hello." I think of my colleagues and myself in the morning. We are running around like crazy: making copies, correcting papers, answering phone calls, going to meetings, getting the materials out for the first activity, and changing the center chart. Then the buses come and we need just five more minutes. Students come into our rooms and see our backs and a quick wave. They are rarely all called by name and met at the door. That old paradigm is now *gone*!

Students are met everyday at the door. Every child's name is said with a "Hello, good morning, hi there," etc. The first thing they do when they come in the room is to make a "Hello" note for someone.

Hello Notes

Each student has a classlist on his or her desk. Each student's classlist starts with a different name highlighted. The highlighted name is the student who will get a "Hello" note. Tomorrow, the next person under the highlighted student will be written to and his/her name will then be highlighted. This process continues until all students have written to each other. Also, by everyone starting at different names, every child will be getting a "Hello" note each morning.

Teri	Clarence
Matt	Tawanda
Pedro	Jamal
Timisha	Dana
Michaela	Chen
Abagail	Jerimiah
Calvin	Belinda
Milan	Aman
Pauline	Saki
Jake	Rafael
Lorena	Tommy
Alex	Jean-Young
Jose	Tyronne
Tameeka	Laura
Selina	Margo

Teri	Clarence
Matt	Tawanda
Pedro	Jamal
Timisha	Dana
Michaela	Chen
Abagail	Jerimiah
Calvin	Belinda
Milan	Aman
Pauline	Saki
Jake	Rafael
Lorena	Tommy
Alex	Jean-Young
Jose	Tyronne
Tameeka	Laura
Selina	Margo

Teri	Clarence
Matt	Tawanda
Pedro	Jamal
Timisha	Dana
Michaela	Chen
Abagail	Jerimiah
Calvin	Belinda
Milan	Aman
Pauline	Saki
Jake	Rafael
Lorena	Tommy
Alex	Jean-Young
Jose	Tyronne
Tameeka	Laura
Selina	Margo

Notice how the three lists above all start with a different name highlighted. Students have five minutes to make and send a good morning note. The reproducible on page 136 can be used to start students off.

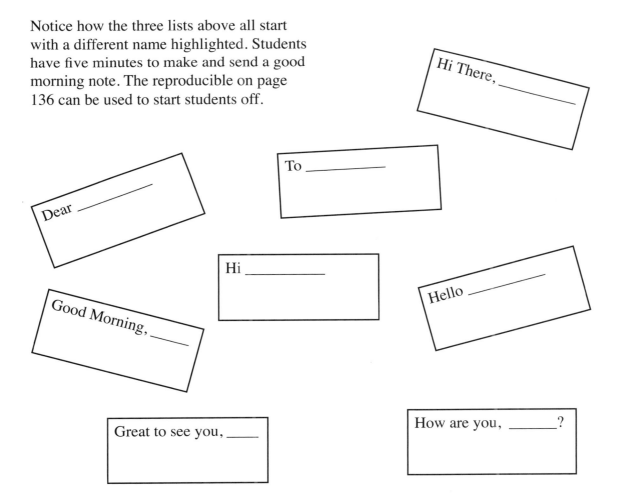

Get Them Up

Eric Jensen says, "Your brain gets a thrill when your body's not still." So the bottom line is that we need to get students up and we need to get them moving. Below are my top five ways to get them up and moving.

Stand Up and Keep Teaching

The act of just standing up increases your heart rate by five to ten percent compared to sitting. This means more blood and oxygen flows to the brain! (Jensen 2003). So as you are teaching, ask students to stand up, then just keep teaching. The students are so funny when I do this. Their whole body language changes. They think they're getting ready to **do** something. Just keep teaching. They are so attentive. Finally someone will ask, "What are we going to do?" My answer is usually, "We're learning about the ocean and waves, aren't we?" They will ask why they are standing. I'll answer, "I don't know. Why don't you sit back down." You just want them up to stretch for a few moments, but don't stop the teaching.

Stand Up and Talk to the Person Next to You

After important concepts are discussed, students will be asked to stand up and talk to the person next to them. Each child chooses the name of an animal. The teacher will then decide who goes first by any of the following options:
> the one whose animal's name comes first alphabetically,
> the one whose animal is smaller,
> the one whose animal is bigger.

The partners who go first play the role of the teacher. Set a timer for two minutes. The "teachers" have two minutes to reteach and explain to their partners what was just learned. When the timer goes off, the roles change. The "teachers" are now the students and must listen to their partners reteach and explain what was just learned.

Change Your Seat

When I think students need to move, I'll stop teaching and say: "You have thirty seconds. Change seats with someone." Once students have changed seats, continue with your teaching.

If this becomes a frenzy time or a time of arguments, then do the following. Every child has a sticky on his/her desk. The stickies are in pairs. For example, there are two pink ones, two yellow ones, two blue ones, two orange ones, two with a red dot on them, or two with a blue dot on them. When students change seats they are to go to the desk that has the same sticky that matches the one on their desk.

Sit on Your Desk

I usually use this strategy when I'm nailing a fact home or we are reviewing an important piece of information. I'll ask students to sit on their desks. I state the piece of information and then they chorally say it back. As soon as I ask a student to repeat what was just said, I can really see their "attentiveness antennas" come out. They never know when I'm going to ask them to repeat something that was just said.

Pass Out Papers and/or Materials

You want to hold back something that students will need for the lesson being taught. For example: scissors, highlighting tape, a map, a handout, etc. When it is time for students to use that item, a new kind of "passing out materials" is utilized.

Choose four children. I usually choose four students who I think are the "neediest" at that moment. They each get ¼ of the materials that need to be passed out. They take the materials and go to the four corners of the classroom.

The following directions are now given to the rest of the class for getting their materials.
1. Get up.
2. Go to the child farthest from you.
3. Call him/her by name.
4. Give him/her a compliment.
5. Receive your material.

Everyone is up and moving, not just the four students who are passing out items. By choosing key students, it's amazing what it does for their self-esteem. I watch children who are having a tough day saunter over to their corners with their heads down. By the time they have passed out the items, they are smiling, their heads are up, and their whole body language says, "I feel better." Being called by name and given a compliment is something that many of our students will not experience except during this time. It's a fabulous movement activity for all students, as well as a self esteem booster for four of them.

Clock Partners

This is a great way for students to have a variety of different partners throughout the school year. It avoids problems about who is whose partner and students always having the same partners. It's also an easy way for students to find their partners quickly.

Students Self-Selecting Partners

Each student is given a clock face with blank lines extending from each hour on the dial.

Each student visits a classmate and they each sign the other's clock at the exact same hour. For example, if Tyrone goes to Alex, then Tyrone will sign Alex's clock at 4:00 and Alex will sign Tyrone's clock at 4:00. When the teacher says, "Please get with your 4:00 partner," Tyrone and Alex know they go quickly and quietly to each other and wait for directions. Each child will have twelve names on his/her clock.

Students could have clock partners from the beginning of school until the December break. When they come back to school in January give them new clocks and choose new clock partners for the remainder of the year. This way, by the end of the year they will have had twenty-four different partners.

Teacher Choosing Partners

Sometimes you may find that you would like to select the students' partners. You could set up your students so they have three different kinds of partners.

1. Partners that are at about the same reading level.

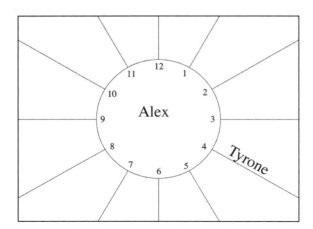

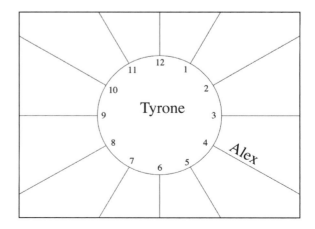

2. Partners who are paired with one being a better reader and the other a weaker reader. Be careful and do not pair students who are too far apart in their reading abilities.

3. Partners who are friends. Reading levels do not matter.

You could also do a combination of teacher selection and student selection. Students could choose odd numbered partners and you choose the even numbered partners; or students could choose partners from 12:00-5:00 and you choose partners from 6:00-11:00.

In the example below, students have chosen their own partners from 12:00-5:00. The teacher has two hour partners of like abilities, two hour partners of different ability levels, and two hour partners of students who need practice working with each other in terms of cooperation. The key is when you organize the clocks and partners, each child must sign his/her partner's clock at the exact same hour, like the Alex and Tyrone example on the preceding page.

There is a clock reproducible on page 137.

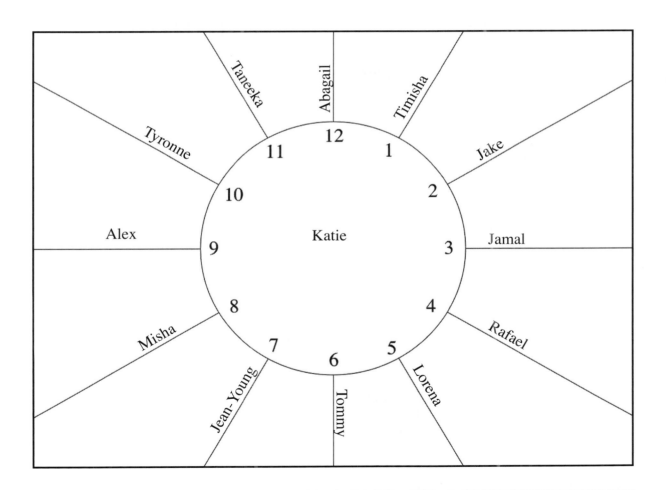

Other Ways to Find Partners Quickly and Quietly

I will admit that having students partner up had never been a favorite activity of mine. There always seemed to be arguing, crying, or complaining. Now, I thoroughly enjoy partner activities because of the organization of clock partners and the following ideas.

Weekly Partners

Partners change every week. Put a name on a sticky note. Put the sticky note on a child's desk on Monday morning. That student is their partner for the week. If you don't use sticky notes, post a class list for students showing their partners for the week.

Neighbor Partners

These partners can be changed weekly, twice a week, or daily. Put words on the board such as: behind, in front of, left, or right. Whatever is written on the board is the partnering option for that day. For example, today's partner is the person to the right. Tomorrow's partner might be the person in front of you.

With the above two partnering systems you have full control of how students are partnered. The next two partnering systems show how students have control or it is "luck of the draw" how students partner up.

Match It Partners

Have a set of card that have two pictures, letters, numbers, or vocabulary words that match. The cards get passed out. Students find the person who has their matching card and they are partners for the week, day, or activity.

Anyone Partners

Students are given four sets of directions. When the music starts:

1. stand up,

2. raise your hand high,

3. find a partner,

4. put your hand down.

Students put their hands up so they can see who needs a partner. Hands being raised help the last couple of students find partners.

Pull Three Names: Answer, Repeat, Repeat

This is an activity that can be used with any curriculum area: reading, writing, math, social studies, science, etc. Use the same can or container with names that were discussed on page 17.

Ask a question and then choose three names from the can. Students do not see the names you have chosen until the end. Choose the strongest learner of the three children to answer the question, the second child repeats the answer, and then the third child repeats the answer. Students never know when they are going to be called. I am amazed at the difference in attentiveness with my students as soon as I bring out the name can. It always keeps them hopping because they never know when their names will be pulled.

The more students hear and repeat information, the greater their understanding. This works especially well with nonfiction texts. Read a paragraph or a couple of sentences. Then pull three names. The three students must repeat the information in their own words. All students are hearing the information four times; once from you and then three more times from their peers.

This is also a great strategy if you are working with definitions. You read the definition from the glossary or dictionary and then pull three names. The three students, one at a time, have to retell the definition in their own words.

Throw a Ball

This activity has a ball being thrown to a student, who then catches it and answers a question that was asked. We often learn a lot by knowing what doesn't work, so let's start with what doesn't work when throwing a ball. I started by throwing the ball to anyone I wanted, but it always put certain students on the spot. There were those who didn't want anything to do with catching the ball because they didn't want to be put on the spot to answer a question. So when the ball was thrown to them, they purposely wouldn't catch it and let it fall right in front of them. All the students around the ball then dove to get it and disaster ensued. There were also students who were making noise to get my attention because they wanted the ball thrown to them.

Now let's look at what works and how throwing the ball is a great strategy.

First: The teacher asks a question. Students who want to answer the question raise their hands. For example, the teacher throws the ball to Philip, who has his hand up, and he answers the question. If the answer is incorrect, the teacher corrects the information. Remember, the ball has been thrown to a child who has raised his hand, so he is saying that he thinks he knows the answer and if he doesn't, he is confident enough in himself to be corrected.

Next: Philip throws the ball to whomever the teacher chooses. That child catches the ball and repeats what was just said. He or she could repeat just the answer or both the question and the answer.

Then: The teacher asks another question. The student who has the ball throws it to anyone who has his or her hand up. That child catches the ball and answers the question.

Last: This cycle continues for as long as you want to ask questions.

So here is what is really happening. You are calling everyone on the carpet to listen and attend, but you're not putting them on the spot academically. My students know I will never put them on the spot and ask them to answer questions if they haven't raised their hands. However, I will always put them on the spot to repeat what was just said. They must always be attending and listening.

If students get the ball thrown to them and do not remember, or were not really listening and need some help, they are allowed three lifelines. Often students do not like to admit they need help, but they do like to ask for a lifeline. Following are three lifelines.

1. The person who just answered the question

The one with the ball is allowed to say to that person, "What did you just say?" or "Tell us again what you just said."

2. Anyone in the classroom

The one with the ball can ask any person in the classroom what was just said.

3. The Teacher

The one with the ball can ask the teacher to repeat the question and the answer.

The most important part of this process is that the one who has the ball and could not repeat the answer *must* repeat the answer after getting the lifeline. There is no such thing as "passing." Students must repeat the answer. So what is happening is this: students who used to sit back, never answer, and not pay attention are now attentive because they never know when the ball is going to be thrown to them.

I knew this activity was working because of a discussion with a student named Sam. Sam is a child who will not tell me he wants to talk to me. Instead, he will hang back when the class is lining up to go somewhere so he can get me alone. We were lining up for lunch and Sam was hanging back, so I knew he wanted to talk to me about something. I sent my students to lunch with a colleague and hung back in the room waiting for Sam to open up. If I ask Sam if he wants to talk to me he'll say, "No" and I'll lose the moment. So I must just hang back and wait patiently until he is ready to talk.

Finally he came up to me and said, "I just love catching the ball!" I thought, "of course you do because you love throwing things." I asked him, "Why?" He said, "I love catching the ball because I always have the right answer." That said it all. Sam rarely likes to talk in the whole group setting because he's a struggling learner. It's not often that he has the correct answer. The Throw a Ball activity has given him the confidence to talk in front of his classmates.

I have found that Sam and my other fragile learners listen very carefully now to the student who is answering the question because they want to repeat the correct answer in front of their peers and get the positive feedback.

If students make any kind of "ooh ooh" noise, they will not get the ball thrown to them. This activity has really helped my students who always make grunts, groans, and noises when they raise their hands.

No one is getting "bored" because they all love catching and throwing the ball. My proficient learners are usually the first ones to raise their hands and my less-abled learners are usually the repeaters.

If you have a piece of information that is very important, you might have four repeaters. Call them by names, "Sam, Jamal, Katlyn, and Tyner. In the order that your names were called, repeat what was just said." Look at how many times students hear the answer. They hear it once when you give the initial information, once from the child who raised his hand and answered the question, four times from four different repeaters and then once again from you as a closing statement. So students hear the information seven times from six different people!

Following is a summary of the Throw a Ball activity.

You ask a question. Throw the ball to someone who has his or her hand up. That student answers the question. The teacher tells that student, #1, to throw the ball to student #2.

Student #2 repeats the answer. Then you ask another question. Student #2 can throw the ball to anyone he or she chooses as long as that student's hand is raised (student # 3).

Student # 3 answers the question. The teacher tells student #3 to throw the ball to student #4.

Student #4 repeats the answer. Then you ask another question. Student #4 can throw the ball to anyone he or she chooses as long as that student's hand is raised (student # 5).

Student # 5 answers the question. The teacher tells student #5 to throw the ball to student #6. Student #6 repeats the answer.

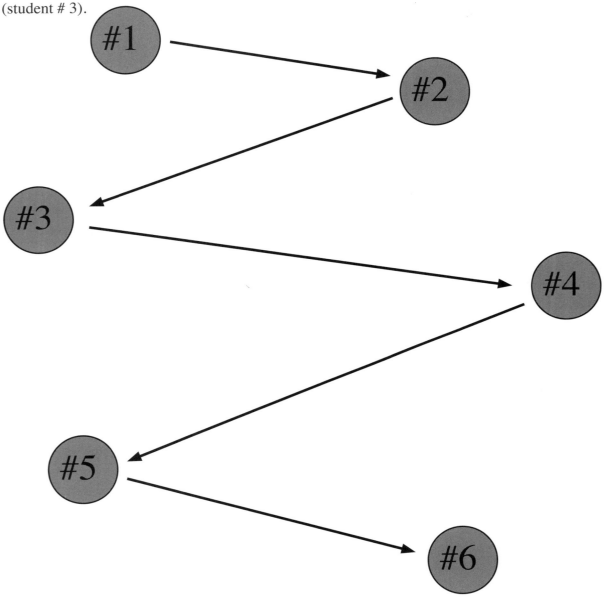

Think Time,
I Forgot,
He Took My Answer

These three issues are all integrally related. Students are raising their hands and saying they forgot what they were going to say, or someone just took their answer. Let's address these three issues, as they are all intertwined.

Think Time

When a question is asked in the classroom, no one may answer for a certain period of time. That means:

> no hands up,
> no noises,
> no jumping out of your seat,
> no calling out the answer.

It means be *quiet* and *think* for fifteen seconds.

My family and I watch Jeopardy many evenings on television. There are so many times when I know the answer but I can't think of it fast enough and I end up making noises like "uh…uh…uh…" or I'm yelling "I know this... I know this … give me a minute." But I don't have a minute to think. I must answer the question in seconds or at least before a contestant pushes his or her button and says the answer, *which I knew*, but didn't have enough think time. This always reminds me of students and what I do to them when I ask questions! So the rule now is, after a question is asked, no one may respond for 15 seconds.

How can you keep track of the fifteen seconds?

Watch the second hand
on your classroom clock.

Use a teach timer
(available at Husky Trail Press).

Play a fifteen second clip of music.

When the fifteen seconds are over, hands may go up. Anyone who makes a noise or calls out the answer will not be called upon. I will often call on Katie first, because it is extremely hard for her not to just yell out an answer. So I can reward and praise the positive behavior by saying, "Katie, thank you for not calling out the answer. What do you think it is?" This has really helped her behavior during whole class instruction time when questions are being asked.

I Forgot

Many students raise their hands after think time. Then, when called on, they say they forgot what they were going to say or they just forgot the answer. Part of this behavior is that students want to put their hands up so they can show all their peers that they know the answer even if they do not. When they get called upon, saying "I forgot" is really a way of passing. So everyone thinks they know the answer, are smart, but just forgot it at that moment.

Here's a strategy for this situation.

Teacher "What is the main idea of these two pages that we've just read?" (Teacher calls on Alisha who has her hand up.)

Alisha "I forgot what I was going to say."

Teacher "Don't you just hate when that happens! I'll ask another person for an answer and then come back to you. If you haven't remembered by then, you can repeat the answer that was just given."
(Teacher calls on Timisha).

Timisha "The main idea is that the peddler is looking for his caps and the monkeys have hidden the caps in the trees."
(Teacher goes back to Alisha)

Teacher "Hi, Alisha. Have you remembered what you were going to share with us?"

Alisha "No, I still can't remember."

Teacher "That's OK. That happens to all of us. What did Timisha just say about the main ideas of these two pages we just read?"

Alisha "That the peddler was looking for the caps that the monkeys have hidden in the trees."

Teacher "Great job, Alisha. You were listening and understand."

Sometimes our very fragile learners want to be acknowledged for knowing an answer. Their hands often go up to shout to the world they have the answer and then they get out of it by "passing." Students know they will never be put on the spot for a correct answer but they will always be put on the spot for a "follow-up" task that is manageable.

He Took My Answer

Another way for students to raise their hands and then pass is by saying, "Someone just took my answer."

Here's a strategy for this situation.

Teacher   "Who can name one type of transportation?"
(Teacher calls on Maria, who has her hand up.)
Maria   "Trains"
Teacher   "Great. Who can name another form of transportation?"
(Teacher calls on Pedro, who has his hand up.)
Pedro   "She just took my answer."
Teacher   "Don't you hate when that happens. Tell us again what Maria said."

Now one of two things will happen. Pedro will repeat what Maria just said and on we go to another question.

But more often Pedro looks at us with an "Oh, no. I don't know what she said" expression. So the conversation would continue like this:

Pedro   "I don't know."
Teacher   "That's OK. That happens to all of us. Use a lifeline"
(remember lifelines from pages 28 and 29).
Pedro   "Marko, what did Maria just say?"
Marko   "That trains are a kind of transportation."
Pedro   "Trains are a kind of transportation."
Teacher   "You're right. Great use of a life line and listening. Who can think of another form of transportation?"

The bottom line is that all students in the classroom are responsible for listening and attending. There is no such thing as passing by saying, "I forgot" or "My answer was just taken." What I find fascinating is that my struggling learners will raise their hands literally a second after I have called on someone because they know I often say, "I'll ask you next." So we set them up to have a correct answer because they can repeat what was just said.

The more repetition, the greater the understanding, and the greater the confidence to speak in front of the whole class.

Call Back Song

One of the biggest time eaters of our day is transition times: cleaning up between assignments, getting ready for specials, cleaning up for lunch, changing from math curriculum to science curriculum, or coming back in from recess. These only name a few of our transition times. There are days when transitions seem to take up to fifteen minutes. I can hear myself saying:

"Let's go."

"Hurry up."

"You have one minute left."

Students, especially young children, are not good with time management. So my saying "You have one minute left," means absolutely nothing. That's where a Call Back Song comes in.

I became aware of this strategy at a workshop put on by Rich Allen. He would give us breaks but never had to ask us even once to come back and get ready to work. He had a Call Back Song. When he played this song, we knew we'd better be in our seats, ready to learn when the song was over. It was amazing. So I tried it with my students. I can say never, and I mean never, did I have to say those above statements: "Let's go. Hurry up. You have one minute left," once I introduced a Call Back Song.

Here's the Call Back Song routine. Anytime you want students to clean up or transition to another activity, play the Call Back Song. Play it loudly at first so all students

hear it. They all have to wave at you so you know they hear the song. Then lower the volume because it lowers their voices. They have to be quiet enough to hear it. Once students have cleaned up, they may not go to their seats if someone is not finished. At this time they are a team. They all work together. No one is sitting down waiting as long as peers are out there cleaning. They all need to jump in and help.

When the song is over, have a stopwatch ready and start it. For every second that you wait for them, they owe a minute of their recess. Now that sounds very strong, but I "fudge it" a bit. Let's say they owe me three minutes of their recess after the first cleanup time of the morning. The next time they need to transition, I tell them if they are cleaned up by the time the song is over, I'll give them back the three minutes and will give them an extra minute of free time. Rarely do they owe me time.

Getting Their Attention NOW

Call Back Songs get students to fully clean up and transition, but there are times when you just want their attention for a moment or two. That's when the following strategies can be used. They are very effective. You start a "ditty," a song, a poem, and the students finish the rest. There you go; you have their undivided attention for a moment. Some fun attention-getters are:

Teacher	Students
Da, da da da da,	da da
Use the above melody, but instead of saying it, clap it out.	clap clap
Zippity doo da	zippity aye
Old McDonald had a farm	E-I-E-IO

Highlighting

This activity works well with whole class reading selections where students all have their own copies of a text. Some examples are science texts, social studies texts, basals, anthologies, and handouts.

Everybody has a highlighting tape card that looks like this. Notice the following things about the card:

1. Each piece of tape is folded back a little bit. This is called the "grab tab." The "grab tab" is where students hold the piece of tape to pull it on and off their pieces of text. Without the "grab tab," students start picking at the tape to get it off the text and then problems occur.

2. There are lines drawn with a marker on each of the strips of paper. This is so you and the students can keep track of their pieces of tape. When a lesson is over, ask students to hold up their highlighting tape cards. It is easy to see where a piece of tape or two is missing when the lines are there.

3. There is a variety of highlighting tape colors on the strip of paper. This is so you can work with more than one concept at a time. Some examples are:

Highlight the main idea in one color and supporting details in another.
Highlight living things in one color and nonliving things in another.
Highlight short vowels in one color and long vowels in another.
Highlight odd numbers in one color and even numbers in another.
The list is endless.

When the tape is used, everyone has to find the answer in the text, not just one or two children, who always just call out the answer. And now, even if some students still call out the answer, everyone has to go back into their books to find it and highlight it.

The tape also works well when introducing new concepts and having students working with the text. Instead of verbally answering or writing answers on a piece of paper, they highlight the answer. And if their answer is wrong-no big deal! Just move the piece of tape and read the correct answer. My students take more risks now with the tape because if they are incorrect, all they have to do is pick up the tape and move it.

This is what the tape looks like before it is put onto the highlighting card. It looks just like a roll of Scotch tape.

I Can't Hear You

Most of the time in the classroom when children give answers, the teacher repeats what was just said. This is really a very subtle way of telling students that they do not have to listen to each other because you will always repeat what someone just said.

We also do not want the excuse of, "I couldn't hear him/her" to be used by others when truly they were just not attending and listening. It is the student's responsibility to let others know if they cannot be heard. If you can't hear someone, do something!

If someone is speaking and students cannot hear what is being said, then the following two ideas can be used:

1. Stand up and look at the child speaking. The child speaking can begin again, ask what was not heard, or decide to stand up and continue with a louder voice.

2. Raise both hands in the air. The child speaking will see hands in the air and know that he/she must try to raise the voice level.

This places the responsibility of hearing and listening on the students themselves, not the teacher.

If the child talking has a **very quiet** speaking voice, then try the following two ideas:

1. The quiet talker will talk to the person next to him/her and then they will *together* chorally answer, ask, or discuss what needs to be said.

2. The quiet child can ask for a lifeline voice to help him/her get the information across in a manner in which everyone can hear.

Both of these ideas have really helped some of my students who are so quiet it is difficult to hear anything they say. This puts them on the hot seat in terms of talking in front of an audience, but it gives them as much support as they need.

Ideas, connections, and implementation strategies.

Chapter

Questioning Window

Preface

While looking through Student Engagement, our first Window of Opportunity, we see that students need to be actively involved in the learning process. Then it follows that they should be equally engaged in the questioning process.

We want students asking questions that promote higher-level thinking and discussions during whole group time. The only way to have them come up with good, thought-provoking questions is number one: to model them, and number two: let them practice by asking the questions.

When students ask questions they are actually differentiating themselves. For example, we were working with a unit on arachnids. Instead of giving students questions to answer, their assignment was to ask three questions. Below are three sets of questions from three different students.

Set One

How many legs does a spider have?

Why do spiders wrap their eggs in a silk web sac?

What are baby spiders called?

Set Two

How many body parts does a spider have?

What do spiders eat?

How long does it take the spider to build its web?

Set Three

I wonder if the spider has a hard time staying on his web during a windy day.

How come the rain and wind don't knock down a spider's web?

I wonder if the spider ever gets tired of having to rebuild his web when a kid knocks it down.

Look at the difference between the sets of questions. The first two are very literal and factual. The last set of questions is more pondering and thought-provoking. Let students write their own questions to go along with your science and social studies units. Sometimes you learn more about what students' understanding and depth of knowledge of a topic is by their questions rather than your own. There is definitely a place in the curriculum for teacher questions and test questions, but let's not use them to the exclusion of students asking questions. We, as educators, ask far too many questions in relationship to our students' inquiries. Researcher Kagan has said that teachers ask about 80 questions an hour while students ask only two.

This goal of this window is to give students the structures, hands-on activities, and strategies they need to independently ponder and ask good, meaningful, powerful questions.

Questioning

He Said,
She Said

This is an activity that gets students asking questions and discussing the characters. The boy and girl figures that are used are wooden, like tongue depressors.

Have students decorate the wooden characters with crayons, markers, yarn, and wiggly eyes. Students used stickers for the faces in the example below.

On the back of each wooden figure is an open-ended question that will go along with any book. Put the wooden boys and girls in a container and you're ready to go. Students take turns choosing a figure and asking the question on the back. They can either answer the question themselves or ask someone in the class to answer. If they choose to have someone other than themselves answer the question, then they must repeat the answer.

I usually find my stronger learners want to ask and answer the questions themselves. My struggling learners want to ask the question but have someone else answer it. That's fine as long as they repeat the answer. Repeating makes them attentive to the answer and also helps increase their comprehension.

The wooden boy and girl figures are available at Crystal Springs Books.

The following are some open-ended question that can be written on the back of the wooden boys and girls. Some of these questions come from the book *Question Prompts* by Pat Pavelka.

What character(s) in this book would get along well with the character(s) in another book?

Compare and contrast a character and yourself.

Compare and contrast two characters.

Who does _____ remind you of? Why?

Who are the minor characters? Why are they important to the story?

Do you think a character behaved responsibly? Why? Why not?

Why did _____ choose _____?

What are a character's strengths?

What are a character's weaknesses?

What is your opinion about _____? Why?

What would you recommend to _____? Why?

Would you have done something differently than _____? Why? Why not?

What were the consequences of _____ actions?

Justify _____ actions.

Describe a character. Back up your description with textual support.

Discuss the problems a character is having.

Does a character change from the beginning of the book to the end? How?

Question Cups

This activity, Question Cups, supports discussions about the other five question words: what, where why, when, and how. The activity, He Said, She Said, for "who" questions is on pages 41 and 42.

Use wooden sticks such as tongue depressors or Popsicle sticks. On the back of each wooden stick, write an open-ended question that will go along with any book. Put the wooden sticks in cups or containers labeled with the question words they relate to and you're ready to go.

Students take turns; first choosing a question word and then choosing a stick. They can either answer the question themselves or ask someone in the class to answer. If they choose to have someone other than themselves answer the question, then they must repeat the answer.

I usually find my stronger learners want to ask and answer the questions themselves. My struggling learners want to ask the question but have someone else answer it. That's fine as long as they repeat the answer. Repeating answers keeps them attentive and also helps increase their comprehension.

The following picture shows some question word cups. Fill the cups with marbles and then put in the sticks. The marbles keep the sticks upright.

Below are some open-ended question prompts for the wooden sticks. Some of these came from the book *Question Prompts*, by Pat Pavelka.

What

What do you think will happen next?

What recommendations would you give to a character? Why?

What is the author trying to tell you in this book?

What did the author have to know in order to write this book?

What experiences in the book are similar to your own?

What would have changed if _____ was different?

What would you have done if…?

If you could change the title, what would it be? Why?

What conclusion can you draw…?

Where

Where does a character get his inner strength?

Where were you confused?

Where did you learn a life lesson?

Where in the story was the character unfairly judged? Why?

Where were you able to predict what was going to happen next? Why?

Compare and contrast the setting to where you live.

Where in the story did you feel a "pit in your stomach" as you read? Why?

Why

Why do you think…?

Why did _____ do _____?

Why is the chapter titled _____?

Predict a character's life five years from now. Why have you made this prediction?

Why do you think the author wrote this book?

How

How would you have changed the ending? Why?

How does the author show a character's belief/value system?

How does a character try to overcome his or her problem?

How is the setting of this book like the setting of another book?

How is the theme of this book like the theme of another book?

How is a character in this book like the character in another book?

How would you explain…?

How would the story be different if…?

When

When did you get an "ah ha" moment? Why?

When did a character have an "ah ha" moment? Why?

When did you have strong feelings as you were reading? Why?

When does a turning point take place in the story? Why?

When did the story take place?
How do you know?

Picture Questioning

Show students a picture. How many questions can they come up with for the picture? The questions cannot be literal questions that can answered "Yes, no," or in two or three words. They must be thought-provoking, pondering, and wondering questions. Sometimes, as you will see in the examples below, students do not ask questions but make judgments based on something they see in the picture. They make connections based on their life experiences.

Following are some of their questions and comments about the picture below.

Do you think the big dog laying down knows the little Pug is there and he's just ignoring him? Why?

Is the big dog pretending to be sleeping so he doesn't have to deal with the pug?

The pug looks like he wants to ask the big dog something. I wonder what that is?

Do you think the pug wants the big dog to get up and play or does he want them to nap together?

They must live in a great home that loves dogs because they are on the couch. My dog is never allowed on the couch.

I wonder if these two dogs live together.

The big dog looks scary because he has his sharp teeth out. But he can't be that scary, otherwise the pug wouldn't go near him.

Where is this taking place? How do you know?

I show students the picture below and it's amazing how their questions, opinions, and predictions change.

Have your students bring in photos from home: their pets, families, vacations, friends, hobbies, themselves, etc., and ask questions. Work with this activity twice a week. Two students each week are responsible for bringing in some kind of picture. It doesn't have to be a photo.

It can be a magazine picture, greeting card, calendar picture, postcard, etc. The photo below is a box of pictures from a second grade classroom. There is paper on the table to the right of the box. Students can write their own questions.

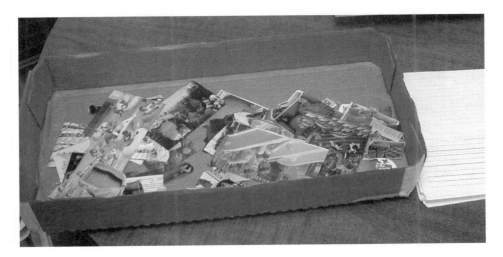

One Good Question Leads to Another

There are three different ways to organize this activity.

Option one (great for individuals)
Each child makes a set of seven arrows.

Option two (great for small groups)
Use a ratio of one set of arrows to four students.

Option three (great for whole group)
One class set for everyone to use.

They can be made out of cardstock, oaktag, cardboard, or any other heavy kind of paper. There are two different sized stencils found in the reproducible section on pages 138 and 139. Some students liked the larger arrows while other preferred the smaller. It's their choice.

Students decorate each arrow. One arrow is the title page and the other six correspond to the six question words:
who, what, where, when, why, and how.

Children get an Albert Einstein quote to put on their title arrow. The quote is found on reproducible page 142. Have discussions about Albert Einstein and his contributions to our world. I wonder how many of his ideas, thoughts, and eventual successes came from asking questions?

On the front of each arrow is a question word with simple, open-ended, one-word prompts to help students formulate questions. These are found on reproducible pages 140 and 141.

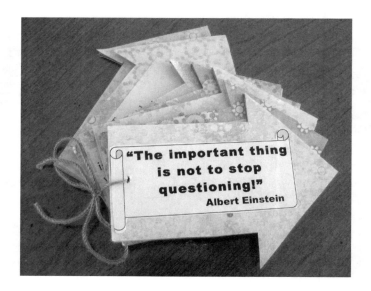

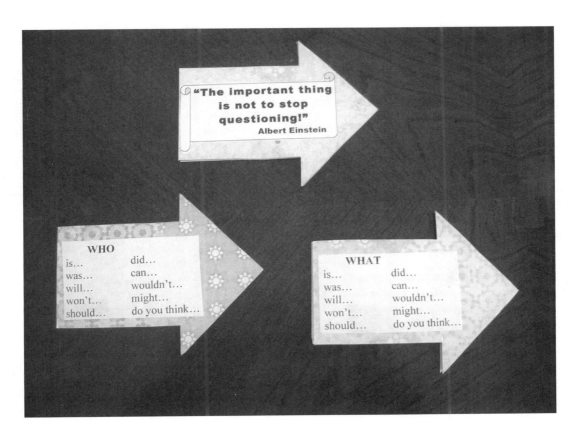

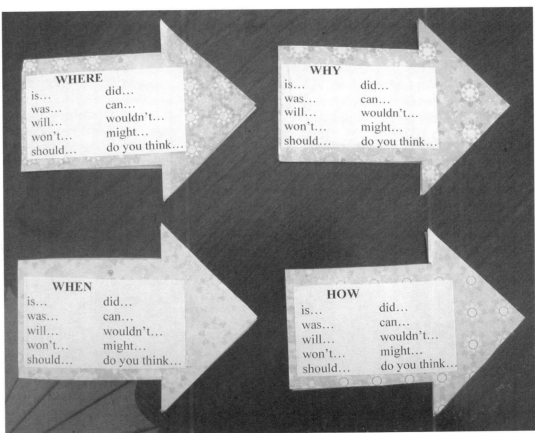

Cubes

Cubes are my students' favorite activity. We use cubes almost every day in some curriculum area. They are easy to use and fun for the children. Virtually any curriculum area can be practiced with a cube, especially questioning.

Below are four different kinds of cubes that are used for our Questioning Window of Opportunity. All of the cubes are found in the reproducible section on pages 143–146.

This first cube is similar to the One Good Question Leads to Another arrow activity found on pages 48 and 49. A student rolls the cube and whatever is rolled, that's the kind of question that must be asked. To get more students involved use the cans with their names (see page 17). The first name pulled is the roller, the second name pulled is the questioner, the third name pulled is the one who answers the question, and the fourth name pulled gives feedback. So with one question and answer, four students are involved! Remember, lifelines are always available.

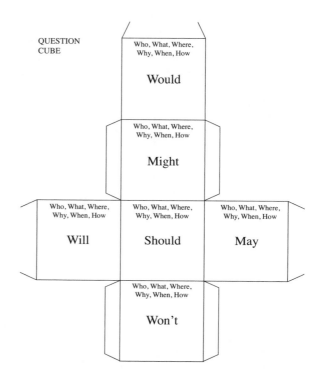

The second cube is an "I Wonder" cube.

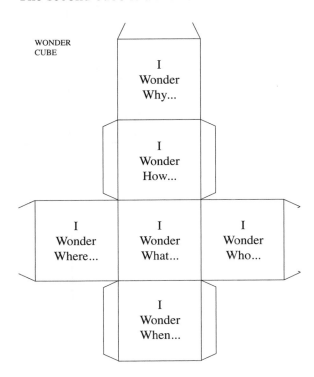

The fourth cube is a nonfiction cube.

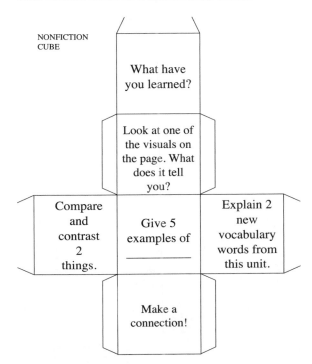

The third cube is a story element cube.

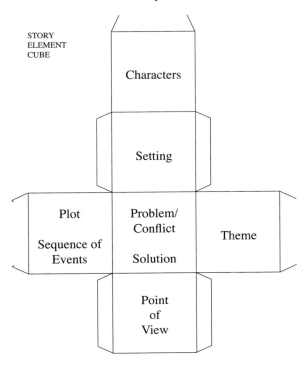

The book *Cubes*, by Pat Pavelka, is full of more cube ideas and has thirteen cubes ready to be assembled.

Shower Liner Grid

For this activity you'll need a shower curtain liner. Using colored masking or electrical tape, divide the liner into sections. See the picture below.

Think about all the times you write items on the board as you teach. As soon as the lesson is over, they get erased. For many of our students it's out of sight, out of mind. Let's change that scenario. Anything you are going to write on the board, write on an index card.

Below is a list of examples from different areas.

Math facts
Spelling words
Examples of parts of speech
Words that start with a specific sound
    or blend
Vocabulary words
Contractions
Science concepts: plants, habitats, weather,
    magnets, etc.
Social studies concepts: land forms, the
    farm, communities, government, etc.
Words instead of "nice"
Punctuation marks
The list is endless.

I rarely write on the board anymore. Anything we discuss gets written on index cards and put into containers. We choose a container based on the curriculum being taught. Students place the index cards on the liner grid.

This is a great way to practice concepts for a test or even to bring up the information two months later to see how well students have remembered the curriculum.

These grids can be played like the Jeopardy game. Each answer has to be in the form of a question. We'll look at an example of a unit on the southwest below.

As these concepts are being studied, they are each written on an index card. You can write a word, phrase, date, name, concept, fact; whatever is appropriate for the unit that is being taught. These index cards are kept in your social studies container. Choose a child to take out the cards and place them on the liner grid.

You can use a number of different students now for just one turn. You'll need two dice.

Student 1 throws one of the die and the number two comes up.

Student 2 tosses the other die and the number four comes up.

Student 3 decides if he or she wants to take the card that is in row two, column four or row four, column two.

Student 3 asks a question based on that card.

Student 4 answers the question.

Student 5 repeats the question and answer.

Five students are involved with just one card.

Connections

Connections are great to use with whole group settings because children naturally differentiate themselves based on experiences, likes and dislikes, and interests. Connections can be used in all curriculum areas: narrative and expository texts, math, reading, writing, science, social studies, art, music, or physical education.

Stephanie Harvey says, "Readers naturally make connections between books and their own lives…they begin to connect characters and issues from one book to another…and they begin to make connections to the larger world." Here are the three connections we will be looking at:

Text-to-Self
Text-to-Text
Text-to-World

This book will not give you the theory and research behind the use of connections, but will show ideas, activities, and strategies to use with your students to help them make connections a natural part of their reading, thinking, and learning. You will also see specific questions that lead students to make deeper connections.

Posters and Bulletin Boards

Connections should be prominently displayed in our classrooms. Following are two poster displays and one bulletin board display using connections. As we read books, stories, poems, and articles together, students write or draw their connections on stickies or scrap paper and we post them.

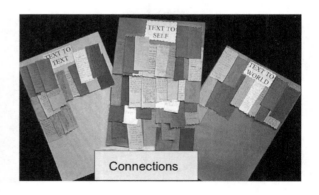

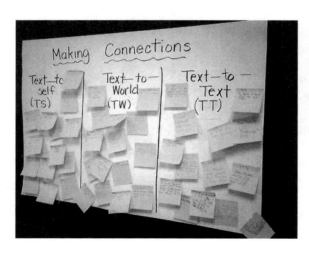

This bulletin board is a year-round display. If I can think of something to put on a bulletin board and keep it up all year, I'm really happy. I don't have to change it every month. When the board is full, the class meets to take down all of the postings. Students talk and reminisce about the books and experiences they have connected to so far in the year.

Text-to-Self

We want students to make connections to themselves and the text. I found that the more general things are, the harder it is for most students to make good, deep connections. The more specific I am, the easier it seems to be for students. The following specific questions help students with text-to-self connections:

Characters

Do you know anyone like the character? How about a Friend? Family member? Classmate? Teacher? Etc.

Do you have anything in common with the character or are you totally opposite?

Would you have done things exactly like the characters? Why? Why not?

Think about the character's strengths and weaknesses. Apply them to yourself or someone you know.

Think about what the characters say and how they say it. Apply this to yourself or someone you know.

Setting

Do you know a place like the setting of the book? Where is it?

How is the setting of the book different from the setting of your life?

Problems

Have you faced any of the problems that the characters are facing in the text? How about a friend? Family member? Classmate? Teacher? Etc.

How would you have handled the problem differently if you were a character? Why?

What feelings are the characters experiencing and when have you experienced those feelings?

Following are examples of students' work with text-to-self connections.

This is a first grade example of a child connecting to *Alexander and the Terrible, Horrible, No Good Very Bad Day*. He made a flipbook. On the outside flaps he glued on the prompt "I can connect with this book!" On the inside he glued the prompt "When I read the part about _____ it reminds me of _____. Page 147 also has a reproducible that students can use to make mini connection books.

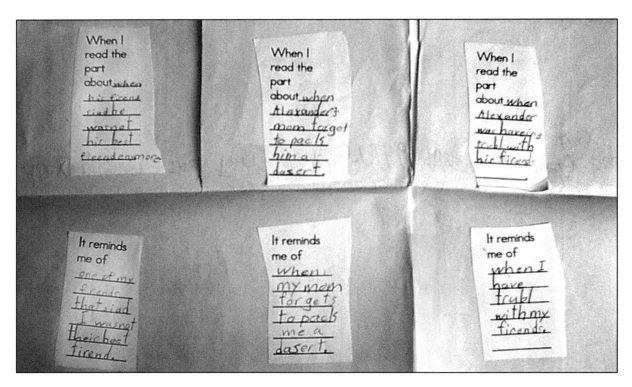

Below are two third grade samples completed after reading the story *The Relatives Came*. This reproducible is found on page 149.

Text Connections

Name:

Hour: The Relatives Came

1. When I read the part when it said they hugged us for hours.

I make the connection When my aunt Linda comes in she hugs me for hours.

2. When I read the part where the guy likes to cut peoples hair.

I make the connection Where in my apartment Audry likes to cut hair.

3. When I read the part were the talk about how big they have grown.

I make the connection Whenever my aunt Jill comes over she talks about how big I'v grown.

Text Connections

Name:

Hour: The Relatives Came

1. When I read the part where the suit cases were packed

I make the connection When I go to my grandma and grampa's hose our suitcases look like that.

2. When I read When they drove on the windey roads.

I make the connection When we drive to or grampa's and grandma's house there is a lot of windey roads.

3. When I read When they had all the people is the yard.

I make the connection When or relatives have a family reunon there is a lot of people.

Text-to-Text

We want students to make connections between characters and issues from one book to another. The following specific questions help students with text-to-text connections.

Characters

Do you know a character from another book that has the same personality as this character?

Does this character have strengths and/or weaknesses that characters from another book possess?

Would a character from a different book have done things exactly like the characters in this book? Why? Why not?

Think about what a character says and how he/she says it. How is it like a character in another book?

Does this character go through changes like a character from another book?

Setting

How is the setting of this book similar to the setting of another book?

How is the setting different than another book?

Problems

Have characters from other texts faced any of the problems that the characters are facing in this text?

How would a character from another book have handled the problem differently than a character from this book? Why?

What feelings are the characters experiencing and when have characters from different books experienced those feelings?

In this section we used questions about characters, setting, and problems to help students make connections. There are more categories to use to help students make specific connections. Other categories may include: emotions, events, actions, plot, and cause/effect.

Text-to-World

This is the hardest connection of all, so we work with this connection differently than text-to-self and text-to-text connections. The ultimate goal here is to have students able to begin making connections to our world as a whole. If you look at a child's world, it is often home and school. It is difficult to make worldly connections when home and school is the extent of your world. So let's start where students are. You start making connections in this flow:

Family and Home
Our Classroom
Our Friends and Neighbors
Our Town and Community
Our State
Our Country
And finally The Whole, Wide, Greater World

Hang up a chart in the classroom that has worldly themes on it. When you are just beginning to discuss text-to-world connections, before they actually read, give the students the world connection. Now as they read, they have to find examples of that theme being used and addressed in the text. Yes, you are giving them the connection, but they must find evidence from the text to support that theme.

The more you work with world connections this way, the more students are able to come up with the theme on their own and give direct textual support from the book to prove it. You'll be amazed at how well students do. My first graders blew me away after using this back door approach. I was always afraid to just give them the answer. However, just giving the answer is not the end. Students must find examples of the theme and, therein, lies the success.

Below is a chart of themes we have used:

Honesty
Tolerance
Survival
Respect
Bullying
Friendship
Loneliness
Responsibility
Kindness
Patience
Courage
Fairness
Acceptance
Rejection

These are trifolds that contain samples of all three kinds of connections. This trifold is in the reproducible section on page 148.

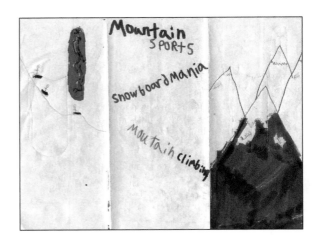

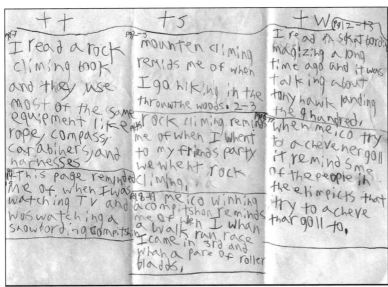

Text to Text	Text to ~~Self~~ World	Text to ~~World~~ Self
Page 135 "British troops, Captain," Ned shouted. In the story Ned Sounds like Paul Revere when he said, "The British are coming!" in Paul Revere's Ride.	Page 90 shows how farmers and almanacs would predict the weather for the seasons to know when to travel and when to plant crops. Like a weatherman on television predicting the weather.	Page 112 shows how hard it is for Tim and his father to walk and to drag the oxen through the snow. It is also hard for me to walk or go places in the snow.
Page 145 "The sword flashed in a bright arc.... Ned's head jumped off his body and popped into the air." This reminded me of the scene in The Patriot where a soldier gets his head blown off by a cannonball.	Page 86 talks about how Redding had shortages of food and supplies during the war and the prices of everything went up, but yet no one was desperate. During the war in Iraq America had shortages of gasoline and the prices went up but also no one was desperate.	Page 75 "Your father doesn't change his mind very often nor easily." Whenever I make up my mind I don't like to change it very easily.
Page 94 shows how Mr. Meeker was beat up by the cowboys on his way to drop off his meat shipment. In the book Holes Kissing Kate Barlow and her band of cowboys went around beating up people and taking their money.	Page 76 talks about how Mr. Heron will pay Tim a shilling to deliver a business letter to someone. Tim was acting as a mailman.	Page 15 shows that Sam doesn't like to follow rules or be told what to do. Sometimes I also don't like to follow rules or be told what to do, especially if I don't agree with it.
Page 39 talks about the Battle of Bunker Hill where the Patriots massacred the British. Also in my Social Studies text book it discusses the Battle of Bunker Hill and how the Patriots won.	Page 75 shows that Tim brought a person a keg of beer and the person tipped Tim. Just like how today someone would tip a waiter, a bartender, or a bagboy.	Page 33 talks about when Betsy asks Tim what side he is on during the war, but Tim is not sure what side he is on. During the war in Iraq a lot of people were for the war or against the war and I wasn't sure what side to be on.
Page 4 discusses how some unknown person shot their pistol at Lexington and a battle broke out, starting the Revolutionary War. This scene was shown in the Movie and book April Morning.	Page 68 says that if an Indian were walking down a road he would get stopped a lot by Police. Today a lot of Arabs because some people think they are terrorists.	Page 12 shows that Tim has a lot of chores to do and he hates doing them. Also I have a lot of chores and I don't like doing them either.
	Page 170 discusses that in the winter a lot of people got sick and everyone was walking around sniffling all the time. This is just like Flu season where a lot of people catch colds.	Page 116 talks about Tim trying to pass the time by trying to name all the countries in the world, but he has trouble naming the small ones and loses count. I also have trouble memorizing and naming a lot of the small countries in the world and get confused.

Ideas, connections, and implementation strategies.

Ideas, connections, and implementation strategies.

3

Chapter

Flexible Grouping Window

Preface

Let's follow the process we've covered so far.

Window One: Student Engagement:
We've taught our grade-level curriculum to the whole class. Ideas, activities, and strategies from the Student Engagement window will help us differentiate as we teach to our whole class so all students can have access to the information.

Window Two: Questioning:
This window helps us involve everyone in the whole class setting by utilizing and applying different questioning techniques.

Now let's move onto Window Three: Flexible Grouping

The whole group approach is usually most effective when working with:

> Grade level curriculum; information that all students at your grade level must be
>> exposed to and have an understanding of,
>
> Read Alouds and discussions,
> Giving directions,
> Modeling and demonstrating activities.

Flexible grouping is at the heart of our differentiated classroom. It is almost impossible to meet the needs of all our students if we use only whole group strategies. We need to vary the kinds of grouping situations in our classrooms in order to support and extend.

- Heterogeneous Small Groups
  These are effective when students are working with cooperative learning, interest-based concepts, and follow-ups to whole group instruction.

- Homogeneous Small Groups
  These work well when students have similar needs of readiness and knowledge in a curriculum area. A group can be brought together who struggle and need more support or a group of students can be formed who need extensions and challenges.

- Quad and Trio
  These groups are often structured with members who are of like abilities, slightly different abilities (some stronger, some weaker), and similar interests.

- Pairs
  These are often structured with two members who are of like abilities, slightly different abilities (one stronger than another), and similar interests.

- Individual
  Students are independently practicing the topics and curriculums you've been teaching and exploring. Window Four, Differentiated Assignments, will give you a wealth of ideas and strategies to use as individual activities.

Students have a lot to say and a lot to share. There is just no way that one teacher can spend enough time individually with each child to hear everything he/she wants to say and share. So let's provide students with opportunities to work, learn, and share with each other. Flexible grouping is an integral part of organizing a differentiated classroom.

Flexible Grouping, here we go...

We Are All Different

We want our students to feel confident about their efforts and achievements. We don't want our students to be so concerned about what the person next them is doing that they lose their own motivation and confidence. Not everyone will be doing exactly the same thing. Not everyone's paper will look exactly the same. We all do things differently and need different strategies and tools to be successful. We have a large banner in the classroom that says:

> Fair is whatever you need to be successful.

Sometimes five students will meet in a small group with the teacher, while three other children work cooperatively together on an activity. There may be four students working in two pairs, while five children are alone at their seats with an independent activity.

For Younger Students

Many times through your day, students may all be doing diverse activities and working in different flexible grouping settings. The following activity has been great to show students that we all do things differently and we all have different needs. Ask students to get a piece of paper and a writing utensil. As soon as these two simple directions are given, all the questions start coming up:

    What kind of paper?
    Lined or unlined?
    Can we use storybook paper?
    Can I use a marker?
    Pencil or pen?

I am amazed at how many questions are asked for two simple directions. Do not answer their questions. Tell them it does not matter. Whatever they use will be fine. After they have something to write on and something to write with give them the following directions: write the names of or draw ten animals. Give no other set of directions. They will probably begin to ask many questions again, but give no suggestions. Just repeat the directions.

When the activity is over, talk about their responses.

    How many drew the animals?
    How many wrote the animals' names?
    How many wrote or drew a dog?
    How many used lined paper?
    How many numbered each item on
       their papers?

There are so many questions that can be asked. Have your students start to ask the questions. When all is said and done, which paper is correct? They all are. Which paper was done the best way? They all were because they were differentiated based on the individual child.

The following are examples from a first grade classroom. Notice all the different levels in one classroom; non-writers to a student who alphabetized her animals.

Below grade level

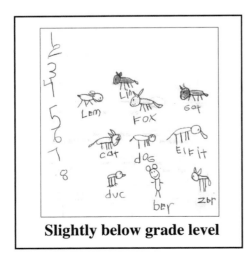

Slightly below grade level

At grade level

Above grade level

For Older Students

Ask students to get a piece of paper and number it from one to ten. As soon as this one simple direction is given, all the questions start coming up:

What kind of paper?
Lined or unlined?
Do we skip lines between each number?
Can I use a marker?
Do we put the numbers in front of or behind the red line on the paper?

I am again amazed at how many questions are asked for just one simple direction: get a piece of paper and put your name on it. When this assignment is completed you discuss their responses.

What kind of paper did you use?
Lined or unlined?
Did you skip lines between each number?
How many lines?
Did you put the numbers in front of or behind the red line on the papers?
How many numbered each item on their papers?
How many circled their numbers?

There are so many questions that can be asked. Have your students start to ask the questions. When all is said and done, which paper is correct? They all are. Which paper was done the best way? They all were because they were differentiated based on the individual child.

Flexible grouping time is a time when you continually bring up the poster prompt: fair is whatever you need to be successful.

Background Groups

Background groups are a great management tool to use during flexible grouping time. Pairs, trios, quads, or any amount of small group membership can meet as a background group. Most of the activities in this Flexible Grouping Window can be done in the background group area.

Basically, a background group is a small group of students who are meeting together without the teacher. My students call themselves "the background group," but have your students name themselves anything they want. The name just states where they are meeting, not what they are doing. The saying, "A picture says a thousand words," is so true. Let's look at two pictures and see what is going on during flexible grouping time.

Below is a third grade classroom. There are three things to note in this picture:

1. The teacher is meeting with a small guided reading group.

2. The background group of five children meeting on the floor in the front of the classroom is working with Book Talk Tubs. Book Talk Tubs are explained on pages 76 and 77.

3. The students at their seats are working on independent work or center work.

Below is a second grade classroom. There are four things to note in this picture:

1. The teacher is meeting with a small guided reading group.

2. The background group of five children meeting on the floor to the teacher's right are silent reading.

3. The students at their seats are working on individual assignments or center work.

4. The two students meeting on the bottom left of the picture (only the back of one of the students can be seen) are reading together.

Partner Reading

There are times when you want your students to read together. You want both students to be actively engaged in the process, while they are the reader and while they are the listener. These are the top six ways students read together in pairs. These suggestions allow reading together to be a fun, enjoyable time, as well as keeping the attention and comprehension levels high. Usually, in this type of partner reading, pairs are of similar abilities. We will refer to the two students in the following scenarios as Student A and Student B. They each have their own text.

Read, Retell, Read, Retell

Student A reads a page while student B follows along in his or her text. Then Student B must retell what happened on the page that Student A just read. If there is confusion or disagreement, both students go back to the text to support answers.

Read, Repeat, Read, Repeat

Student A reads a page while student B follows along in his or her text. Then Student B rereads the exact same page that Student A just read. This really helps with fluency. When Student B rereads, Student A does not follow along but just listens and critiques the voice, inflections, and articulation of Student B. If the book has pages with short amounts of text, then Student B rereads the whole page. If the book is a novel, then Student B chooses and reads only one to two paragraphs.

Chorally

Both students read the page together.

Pass the Reading

Student A starts the reading and then passes the reading to Student B at any time. The reading can be passed by a hum, whispering of the partner's name, a tap, or any other soft, quiet way. Ask students not to pass in the middle of a sentence or at the end of a page.

Readers Theatre

This strategy is done only after students have read the story at least one time through. Each child chooses a part or two, based on how many are needed. After the story has been read together once, each child will work alone. Using highlight tape, partners will highlight the parts they need to read. The story is then read like a play. The hardest part here is for students not to say, "Mr. Pip said" or "Mom said" but just read the dialogue.

Silently

Both students read the selection silently and then ask questions at the end of each page.

See reproducibles on pages 150-151 for a cube and deck of cards to use with this activity. Students will roll the cube or pick a card. That decides how the page, paragraph, or book will be read.

With some modifications, these strategies also work well with groups of three and four students.

Page 150 has these six options on a cube. Students roll the cube and whatever is rolled is how they read the text.

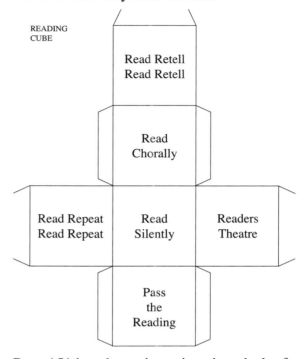

Page 151 has these six options in a deck of cards. Students mix-up the cards and turn one over. This card tells how they read the text together.

Read Retell Read Retell	Read Repeat Read Repeat
Read Chorally	Readers Theatre
Read Silently	Pass the Reading

Mixed Groups: Finding Answers and Textual Support

After working with texts in your basal or anthology, you usually want some follow-up work completed by students. When giving a whole class assignment, the same things continually seem to happen.

Strugglers don't know where to begin so they often become behavior problems. The child who doesn't understand is misbehaving. So how do you increase the understanding, which increases the motivation, which increases appropriate, attentive behavior?

The proficient learners are done too quickly. They often rush through the work giving surface level answers. They are not digging below the surface to achieve the critical thinking and thought-provoking questions and answers they have the potential to give.

Put students into heterogeneous groups or "friend" groups of three to four. Students reread the text together and answer specific questions that were given. They work together as a group. In the picture below, students are reading together.

In this picture, the same students are
looking at questions that were given.
Students each have a white board on their
laps. Although they can discuss the answers
together, everyone must turn in their own
pieces of writing. In this case the writing is
on white boards.

These three students have their basals on
the floor with them. They are discussing
answers and finding textual support in the
book before they go back to their seats
and write.

In past times, I hadn't wanted my students to talk about comprehension questions before they answered them in writing. I did not want them giving each other the correct information.

However, if students do not understand what was read, then you *do* want them to discuss before they write. Otherwise, an incorrect answer will be written. Once they have written the answer incorrectly, you now have two problems. The first is that incorrect information has become more embedded in their heads because it was written; and secondly, you must find time to individually help students understand the information and correct their mistakes.

I encourage students, as they are discussing, to use highlighting tape to highlight the textual support in the book that backs up an answer. Now, when they go back to their seats to write, they have support for each question because text has been highlighted. It's really funny to watch the dynamics during this activity. I'll tell students they have five minutes to discuss the story and the comprehension questions. Students are incredibly attentive and motivated because they know if they work together they will find and mark all the answers to the question. When they get back to their seats the writing is, as one of my students stated, "a piece of cake."

Three to Teach and Reteach

This strategy helps work through the problem of absenteeism. When certain students are absent, it is really a big problem. How and when do you make time to instruct and show what was missed? This is a strategy that involves a trio of learners: one child that has been absent, one very strong learner, and one struggling learner. My students have called this a 3T Club. When students come back from being absent, they will often loudly announce at the door, "I need a 3T Club today." What students do not realize is the reteach part of this strategy.

Remember, there are three members in this group. See the example below.

Katie, the student who was absent:
Katie needs direct instruction of what she missed.

Quentin, a strong learner:
Quentin will act as the teacher. Since he understands the concept well, he will introduce, give examples, and teach what Katie missed.

Amanda, a struggling student:
Amanda has been asked to work with Quentin to help teach and explain to Katie what she missed. Actually, Amanda really needs a reteaching of the information, but instead, she sees herself as the teacher. I've seen huge confidence gains when I ask a struggler to be part of the 3T Club.

Book Talk Tubs

Book Talk Tubs are tubs that students use when they are meeting and sharing thoughts, ideas, and questions about books and texts. Sometimes the tubs have different focuses. Following are examples of three tubs. You will see that each tub has a different curriculum area or concentration for students. You will also see that the tubs may be used for different reading levels, from beginning readers through novel readers.

Reading for an audience and fluency

This Book Talk Tub is being used by students who are reading the story The *Little Red Hen*. The book is written as a play. First, students will each take a card out of the box which will tell them what part they are to play and/or read. They can read the book through as a play with no movement.

They could actually act out the play and add some of their own lines to the story. They could use the puppets in the box to act out the play as they read the exact text from the book.

High-level questioning techniques

This Book Talk Tub is being used by students who are reading the book *The Littles*.

In the tub is the One Good Question Leads to Another activity found on page 48. Also in the tub, on the left side, is a step book of open-ended question prompts that can be applied to any book. You could use the prompts found on pages 42, 44 and 45.

Making connections

This Book Talk Tub is being used by students who are reading the book *Dolphin's First Day: The Story of a Bottlenose Dolphin*. In the tub are the connection prompt ideas from pages 54–60.

These three papers are stationary I found at an office supply store. They are great for connection visuals. The Text-to-Self paper has children all around as a border. The Text-to-Text paper is a scroll. The Text-to-World paper has clouds.

Book Talk Tubs can be used for anything you think a group of students need: support or extensions of concepts. You can have mixed ability groups or homogeneous groups, depending upon what the desired outcome is.

Ideas, connections, and implementation strategies.

Chapter

Differentiated Assignments Window

Preface

Our classrooms have an increasingly diverse population. Children come to us with many different learning styles, interests, experiences, and abilities. Workbook pages and worksheets are not multi-leveled. All students working on the exact same pages and expecting the same outcomes is not differentiating assignments. Students need opportunities to apply and utilize skills and information at their own levels and in their own ways of understanding. Our goal for students is to: show what you know!

Remember from the Flexible Grouping Window, not all students will be working on assignments at the same time. You may have a group with you, four students in the background group using a Book Talk Tub (see pages 76 and 77), three students working in a Three to Teach and Reteach setting (see page 75), or two students Partner Reading (see pages 70 and 71). This window of opportunity gives specific ideas and activities to use when you and your students are working with different flexible grouping options, and you need to give assignments to the rest of your class.

You do not need to plan many different assignments for the many different levels in your classroom. All students can complete these assignments in a variety of different ways.

The assignments in this window allow students to be actively engaged in meaningful work at their ability levels. These assignments can be applied to almost any book, skill, or curriculum area being studied.

There are two parts to this window. The first part discusses all the management issues that come along with differentiated assignments: interruptions, questions about directions, needing help, and what do I do when I'm done? The second part of this window gives specific differentiated assignments.

Differentiated assignments, here we go...

Modeling

MANAGEMENT

One of my biggest mistakes in the classroom is not modeling enough. I show the students how to do something once, and then expect them to do it **alone** and **correctly**. After teaching a lesson, I ask if students have any questions. They all look at me and shake their heads, "No." I ask if they are all set to start work: know what to do and how to do it. They again just look at me and nod their heads up and down. Why is it, then, within one minute of sending them out for independent work, I have a line attached to me of at least three children? I have learned from my mistakes. Modeling is a key foundation of this window.

Modeling plays an integral part in how successfully and easily students are able to complete assignments. There is a specific modeling process that I now follow with all assignments that students will be working on throughout the year. Below are the five steps that we engage in before ever sending students out on their own to complete an assignment.

Step One

The first rule during modeling time is that students must be out of their seats! As soon as I tell them I'm going to model something for them, they are excited and motivated because they can get up. They are allowed to do one of three things: sit on their desks, stand anywhere in the room as long as I can see them, or sit on the floor next to me. I model what the activity involves. Students do nothing but watch me. They can ask questions. I may ask them some questions. But basically, the teacher is doing all of the work and students are just watching. Make sure you do a lot of *think alouds* during this process. Let students hear what is going on in your head. If you're the kind of person that talks to yourself, like I do, this will be easy for you.

Step Two

The teacher still does all the work but now gets most of the answers and feedback from students. Students have taken control of what the assignment will entail and how to do it, but you are still the scribe. You are also working through problems that may come up with that assignment, asking students what they would do if this happened? What if they got stuck? Where could they go for help? Etc.

Step Three

Students are given the assignment but they must work with a partner. See the ideas for partnering on page 27. The reason for partnering is that when students have questions, they will **not** go to the teacher but to their partners. Both partners must turn in the work. One partner cannot do it for both. At this point, do not be concerned if their answers are similar. Yes, they may be copying, but we will deal with that in the next step.

Step Four

Students are given the assignment again and they must still work with a partner. Here is the difference; both partners must turn in different answers/work. Students are now going to learn how to give ideas, hints, and help. There is a big difference between sharing ideas and copying. You want your students to share ideas, help each other when they are stuck, but *not* copy each other. The rules are: you may not touch another person's paper and you may not copy word for word.

The following is an example of what happened during worktime when students were given an assignment The assignment was to list ten breakfast foods. Vincent, a weaker learner, and Carina, a stronger learner, were partners. Carina told Vincent they should first number their papers one through ten, so that's what they did. Then Carina wrote orange juice next to number one. Vincent started complaining because he couldn't write orange juice, that would be copying, but he couldn't think of anything else to write. Carina asked him to think of another kind of juice. He immediately said, "Grape juice." The look on his face was great! He had thought of that answer all by himself with just a little prompt.

Carina then wrote Corn Flakes next to number two. Vincent started his complaining again because he couldn't write Corn Flakes. That would be copying and he couldn't think of anything else to write. Again Carina very quietly and calmly said, "Vin, chill out. Just think of another kind of cereal. You can't write Corn Flakes but what else could you write instead?" You should have heard Vincent. He said, "Oh, I get it. Fruit Loops, Frosted Flakes, Lucky Charms."

Below are their two papers. You can see that most of Vincent's answers came from a hint from Carina's paper.

1. orange juice	1. grape juice
2. Corn Flakes	2. Fruit Loops
3. pancakes	3. waffles
4. bacon	4. sausage
5. butter	5. jelly
6. muffin	6. donut
7. oatmeal	7. hot apple sauce
8. blueberries	8. strawberries
9. grapefruit	9. apple
10. toast	10. raison toast

I'm amazed at how quickly my students picked up on this routine; that sharing ideas is not the same as copying. My students give each other hints all the time when they are stuck instead of lining up at my small group table. They give each other ideas and help for writing topics, spelling, math, you name it. The difference is you have taught them *how* to help rather than copy.

Step Five
Students are given the assignments to complete independently. If they need help, they are to visit a peer and get help and hints.

There are sticky labels, like return address labels, in the classroom that say

      Idea shared by _____.

If a student gets help from someone, give him or her credit for it. My students love to share now because of these labels. There is a reproducible of these labels on page 152. It is set up so you can print it right onto return address labels.

Where Do I Go for Help?

MANAGEMENT

In the preceding strategy, we talked about modeling and how students are taught to help rather than copy. This is a great strategy that has huge success stories and creates that independence we are looking for while working with small groups. However, there was an issue that came up which we needed to address. The same three or four students were always being asked to help. Instead of the line forming at my small group table, the line formed at Jacob's or Saisha's desks. We had to come up with a strategy that would allow students to collaborate and receive help from each other, yet not always have the same students interrupted for help.

Everyone makes a red light/green light circle. Students trace something circular on a piece of red paper and on a piece of green paper. Everyone's circles do not have to be the same size. It's fun to watch students search the room to find something circular to trace. They have used my coffee cup, a plate, a pencil holder, or a container in their lunch box. They glue the red side to the green side.

When they enter the room in the morning, all students put their green sides up on their desks. That means they are available for help and questions. Students are allowed to help two peers. After they have helped two peers, they must turn their circles over to the red side, which means *stop*. If the red side is showing, that child cannot be bothered or interrupted for help or questions. This has made a big difference for two reasons. First of all, it's not the same students who are always interrupted. Secondly, students are going to other children in the classroom that they might not have necessarily visited for help, but they are the only ones with green lights showing.

I even have a red light/green light that I wear as a very attractive necklace. I punched a hole in the circle and put a piece of yarn through it. During small group time I turn my necklace to the red side, which means I cannot be interrupted. This visual really makes a big difference. I watched some of my students. The second I sent them off to work they ran up to me with questions. I don't even think they thought about the assignment. It was just a habit of coming up to the teacher. Now, I've had children start to walk up to me, see the red light necklace, and turn right around looking for someone with a green light showing.

I'm Done, Now What Do I Do?

MANAGEMENT

This phrase does not exist in my room anymore! My mistake was to give students "free choice" when they were finished with their work. So most of them rushed through their work just to get a free choice, leaving many mistakes and unfinished work for tomorrow. And the ones who needed "free choice" the most, never got it because they never finished their work. The following two poster ideas have changed this situation: I Think I'm Done and I'm Done With My Work.

I Think I'm Done Poster

This is a poster that is hanging on the wall. It gives very specific things for students to look for and add to their work. I find if I'm too general with suggestions, students do a poor job proofreading and adding to their work. For example, if I tell a student to add more to his or her paper, I usually get the words, "really" and "very". So instead of the sentence, "He is nice," I get, "He is really, very, very, nice." The more specific you are, the easier it is for students to add quality additions and changes to their work.

Following is the I Think I'm Done Poster. Notice how it starts very easy and gets progressively harder. You could color code this poster. For example, use red marker for the first five items on the poster. Use blue marker for the next two items. Use purple for the next, and so on. You could now tell a student that he must complete all items

through the first two colors. Another child could be told that he must do the red items. It's an easy way to differentiate for the different abilities in your classroom.

> My name is on my paper.
> I used 6 colors in my drawing.
> I have 10 items/things in my picture.
> I have labeled 5 items.
> I wrote one sentence.
> I wrote three sentences.
> I wrote five sentences.
> Add a sentence at the beginning of your text.
> Add a sentence at the end of your text.
> Add 2 sentences in the middle of your text.
> Get rid of nice, really, very, said.
> Add three words to describe your character.
> Describe your setting using the five senses.
> Add dialogue in your text.
> Have one of your sentences end with an exclamation mark.

This poster can grow all year. As you teach new concepts, add them to the chart. This is a reproducible on page 153 that can be passed out for students to have their own copies.

I'm Done With My Work Poster

This is also a poster that is hanging on the wall. It can be used with all subject areas.

When students have completed their work, they can use this chart for any subject area. Basically, students are utilizing and applying whatever they are learning in the curriculum. When students are working during science period and have completed the assigned task, they move to this chart and work with the science topic. When you are working with your math curriculum and students have finished their assignment, they move onto the math topic on this chart. This can be used all day long with whatever topic you are working on when students have completed assigned work.

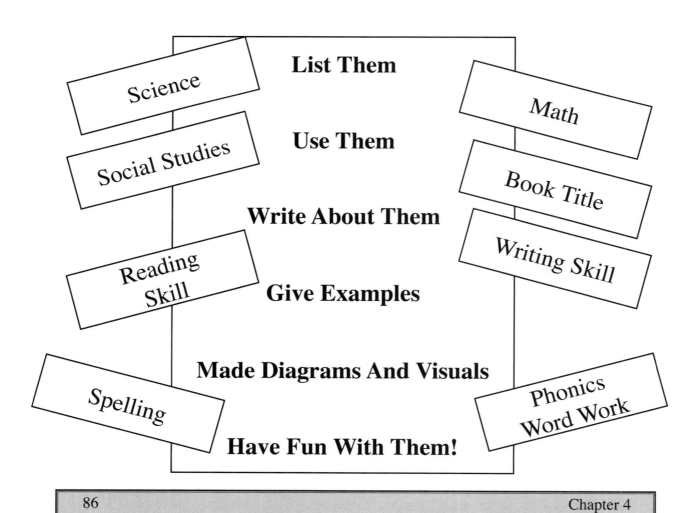

List Them

Use Them

Write About Them

Give Examples

Made Diagrams And Visuals

Have Fun With Them!

Science

Social Studies

Reading Skill

Spelling

Math

Book Title

Writing Skill

Phonics Word Work

ABC Books

ABC books are great resources to use with any ability level, any grade level, and any curriculum area. ABC books can be a center that never changes. Students can be working on books in the following areas:

ABC Books for Beginning Sounds

ABC Books for Read-Alouds

ABC Books for Guided Reading Stories

ABC Books for Science

ABC Books for Social Studies

ABC Books for Skills

The list is endless. Let's look at some children's samples.

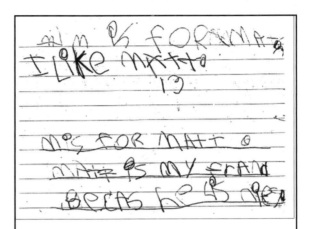

M is for Matt
I like Matt
M is for Matt
Matt is my friend
Because he is nice

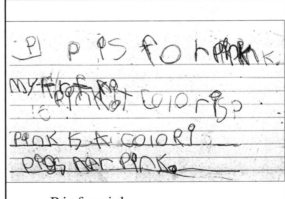

P is for pink
My favorite color is pink
Pink is a color
Pigs are pink

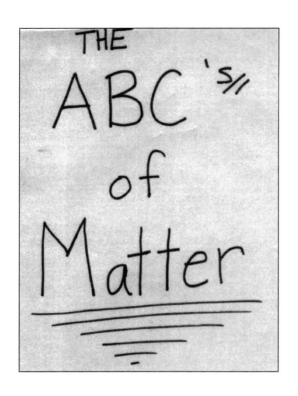

BitS – All matter is made of tiny bits called atoms. when bits of atoms join They make molecules.

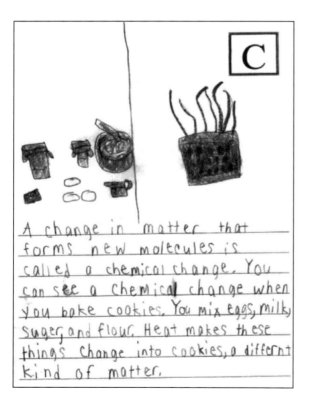

A change in matter that forms new molecules is called a chemical change. You can see a chemical change when you bake cookies. You mix eggs, milk, suger, and flour. Heat makes these things change into cookies, a differnt kind of matter.

Evaporate means to change from a liquid to a gas caused by molecules speeding up from gaining heat. Evaporation means to change from a liquid to a gas.

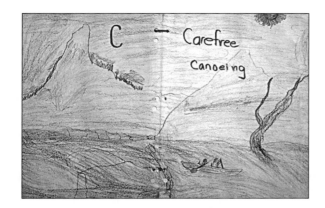

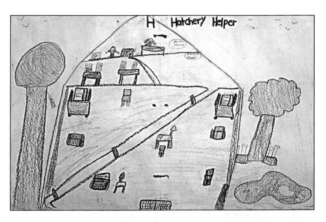

My Name
Your Name

This is one of my student's favorite assignments at all grade levels. They love using each other's names and pictures. Every student needs an envelope with his or her name on it. In the envelope are pictures of the student that were run off on a copy machine. Also included are copies of the child's name run off a number of times. See the picture below. These envelopes are all kept in a plastic tub or box.

Now let's look at all the ways you can use these name envelopes. You'll see ideas for young, emergent readers and writers, as well as ideas for older, more mature readers and writers.

Concentration

Students can play concentration matching any of the following:

Picture	to picture
First name	to picture
First name	to first name
First name	to last name
Gender	to gender

Greater than or less than letters in the name

Greater than or less than syllables in the name.

Compare/Contrast

Students can compare and contrast any of the following:

Number of letters in the names (See the example below. This reproducible is found on page 154).

Fewer Letters Than My Name	The Same Number of Letters as My Name	**More** Letters Than My Name

Number of vowels in the names
Number of consonants in the names
Number of syllables in the names
Boys names to girls names
Names with short vowel sounds to names
with long vowel sounds

Letter Scavenger Hunt

Students need to write their names across or down a piece of graph paper. Younger students have to find words that have the same letters as their names do. Older students have to find vocabulary words from their science or social studies units. The words do not have to start with the letter. The letter just has to be somewhere in the words they find. The younger students seem to want to find words that begin with the chosen letter, where as the older students do not. See the two examples below.

M	i	c	h	a	e	l
mom	ice	cream	horse	a	egg	let
men	igloo		help	at	end	love
many				an		
moo						

M	i	c	h	a	e	l
filament	positive	electron	path	static	electric	particles
	circuits	charge	switch	atoms	neutrons	neutral
				attraction	negative	flow

Math Concepts
Add Names
Gabriella + Emily =

Subtract Names
Michaela – Tony =

Word Problems
Judi and Johanna went for a walk. They met Juan and Kyllie, who had their three younger siblings with them. They all went swimming. How many children were swimming?

Fractions
Fractions of vowels to consonants
Sam has 2/3 consonants and 1/3 vowels. Samantha has 5/8 consonants and 3/8 vowels. 5/8+3/8=8/8

Percentages
What percentage of vowels to consonants does a name have?

Rounding Off
Using first and last names, round off the number of letters to the nearest ten.

Writing Ideas
Letters
Choose a name and write a letter to that person.

New Chapter
Write a new chapter to a book you are reading that includes you and at least one other friend from the classroom.

This only touches the tip of the iceberg when it comes to activities that can be done with names. Your students will come up with exciting, incredible ideas; ones that you've never even thought about!

Poetry Books

This is a center that addresses a number of different content areas as well as reading strategies:

Comprehension of facts and information related to science

Comprehension of facts and information related to social studies

Poems about seasons and holidays

Poems that correspond to certain phonetic and spelling concepts

Tracking for emergent readers

Fluency work for developing readers

Students each have a composition notebook, spiral notebook, or a pocket folder with brads in the middle.

The poems often start out in a whole group setting, move to a flexible grouping setting, and finally become an independent assignment. Before it becomes an assignment at the poetry book center, the text must be worked within some kind of grouping situation.

Introducing the text before students use it at the poetry book center

All students are given the text during a whole group lesson, or it is written on a piece of chart paper for all to see. Poems are read chorally, silently, aloud to a partner, aloud to the whole class by different volunteers, or by the teacher. Students who need repeated reading and more support with the text will use it in some kind of small flexible group setting such as the following.

Small group meeting with the teacher for about ten minutes,
Partner reading: see pages 70 and 71,
Background group: see pages 68 and 69,
Three to Teach and Reteach: see page 75.

Poetry Book Center

The poetry book center can be used a number of different ways.

Option One

Students get a copy of the poem that was used during whole group instruction. They decorate the poem and draw a visual to go along with it. The poem gets practiced at the center either silently or with a partner. The cube, explained on page 70 and 71, works very well with partners reading the poem together.

Option Two

Students do not get a copy of the poem to keep. They copy the poem from the chart. After writing the poem, they decorate it, draw a visual, and practice using the same ideas as option one.

Option Three

The poem has words left out for students to personalize the text. It becomes similar to a cloze activity. Sometimes they use a poem in its original form, but then turn it into a cloze activity at the center. Both options one and two can be applied.

Option Four

There are easy and challenging texts available for students to use. I have proficient readers and writers who always work with option four. They use the poem of the week and then choose one to two new ones to add to their books. There are also students who struggle with the text that was introduced in a whole group. They use an easier text that applies to the same concept or theme they're working with in whole group. Usually students have been introduced to and worked with those easier texts in a small flexible group setting.

Sometimes the directions are to first work with the poem introduced during the whole group instruction. Students must then choose a second text to work with at the center.

Songs relating to concepts and information being studied are also a good resource to use for this activity.

Below is a list of teacher resource books for poetry.

A Poem A Day
    by Helen Moore
American History: Building Fluency Through Practice and Performance
    by Timothy Rasinski & Lorraine Griffin
Partner Poems for Building Fluency
    by Bobbi Katz
Poems for Math Practice
    by Laureen Reynolds
Poems for Shared Reading
    by Karen Sharpe
Poems for Sight-Word practice
    by Laureen Reynolds
Poems for Word-Family Practice
    by Laureen Reynolds
The Big Book of Classroom Poems
    by Kathleen Hollenbeck
The Big Book of Pocket Chart Poems
    by Linda Ross
Most of the above books can be found at Crystal Springs Books

Below is a list of children's literature poetry books.

Big, Bad and a Little Bit Scary
    by Wade Zahares
Burst of Firsts
    by J. Patrick Lewis and Brian Ajhar
I Invited a Dragon to Dinner
    by Chris L. Demarest
Laugh-eteria
    by Douglas Florian
Readers Theatre
    by Robyn Reeves, Laurence Swinburne, and Jack Warner
You Read to Me, I'll Read to You
    by Mary Ann Hoberman and Michael Emberley
Most of the above children's literature can be found at Husky Trail Press LLC

Write About It

This is a great center for creative writing and descriptive paragraphs. This assignment refers to a tub of pictures and a chart on the wall. The chart is there for students who need help getting started. Sometimes the hardest part is starting the task. We often have students who just sit and do nothing. They are not being disruptive or bothering anyone. They are sitting there "thinking." This chart has made a huge difference for these students.

You will find your students who are great writers and have no difficulty starting will not really use the chart. They may look at it, get an idea or two, and then they write on their own. You'll see this in some of the samples that are coming up. The chart looks like this:

Write What You See!

What is in your picture?

Where is your picture taking place?

Look at the colors in your picture.

Notice the different sized items in your picture.

Find different numbers of items in your picture: two dogs, one stump, etc.

What does your picture remind you of?

What connections can you make to your picture?

What does your picture make you think about?

This second grader redrew the magazine picture.

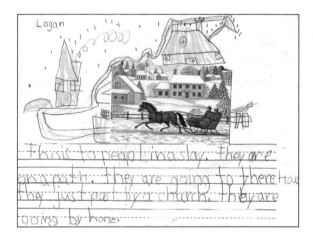

I see puppes. They are in the forist. they are white and brown black to. They're are two puppes They are in the forist on a stumpe they are the same siyea.

This second grader used the actual Christmas card as part of his picture.

Logan

Thris is to peap in a slay. They are on a path. they are going to there Hous they just past by a church. They are going by horse.

These two fourth graders wrote about a picture of two horses in a pasture.

Matt. B

This is a picture of two hourses There is a little houres and a big houres. The little houres is brown and the big houres is black. They have big tails and big ears.

Amy

In the picture there is a mare and a foal. The foal is brown and the mare is gray, black, brown, and white. They both have wiskers. Thrire verry close to the forest. Both mare and foal have lardge ears, and long legs. The horses are both verry beutiful.

Shape Books

Shape books are always tied to your science and/or social studies curriculum. Each day when you are finished with your science and/or social studies period, you should always review what they've learned. Before beginning, you all move to the shape book center to utilize a chart that is hanging on the wall. When you review, write all the items that were taught that day on the chart paper. When students are working at this center, they must "show what they know" in regard to the topics on the chart. The chart can contain: dates, names, facts, vocabulary words, and phrases.

There are three different ways to organize this center. Sample are shown on the next two pages.

Option One

Provide five or six different stencils for students. Students will trace the stencils onto two pieces of paper and cut them out. These are the front and back covers to their shape books. Depending upon students' abilities and choices, they can either cut out more of the same shape for the inside pages or use precut lined paper for the inside pages. The pig sample on the following page is from a child who traced the stencil for her covers as well as her inside pages. The science unit she is working on is the farm. Can you figure out what vocabulary word she is using from the chart? *(produce)*

Option Two

Sometimes I have found great "run-offs" for this center. A picture that can be copied on the copy machine for students is called a "run-off."

The bunny run-off on the following page was used when we were working with a unit on the farm.

We were working with endangered animals when we used the eagle run-off shown on page 98.

Option Three

There are students who do not want to use the stencils. They want to create their own fact book. The fourth grader's sample, shown on page 98, is from a unit on the ocean. This student wanted to put together a mini report with diagrams and pictures. He did not want it to be in a shape.

Option 1

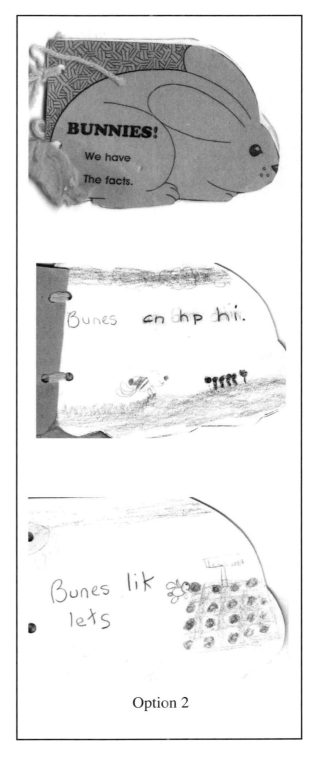

Option 2

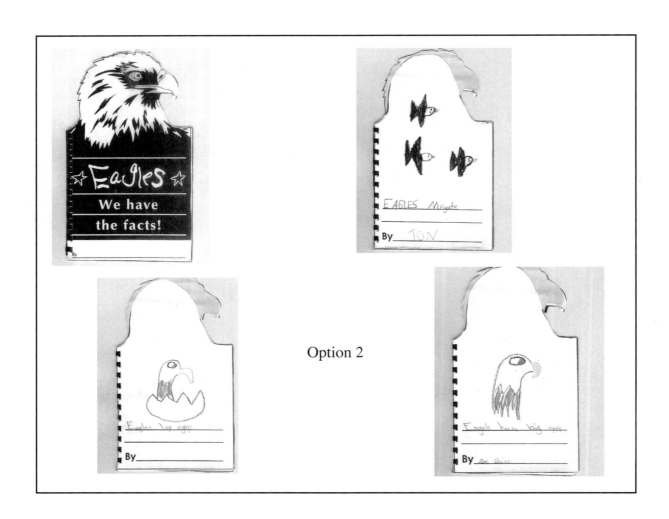

Option 2

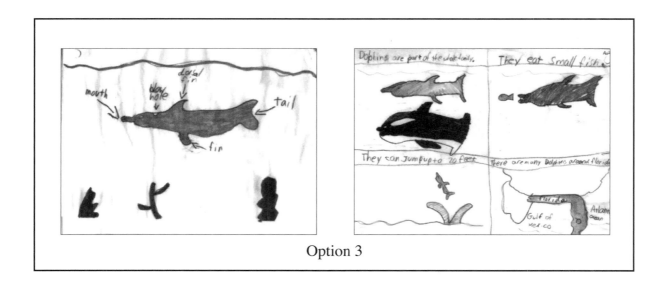

Option 3

Writing to Prompts

ASSIGNMENTS

This assignment can be coordinated with almost any area: children's literature, science, social studies, holidays, daily life, etc. Each week a prompt is given for students to write about. In your classrooms you have students who are at various ability levels in their writing development. Some are great writers, while other are still not sure of letters and sounds, so their comfort level in writing is with the use of pictures.

Create a writing poster that is color coded for students. Each of the lines on the following chart is a different color. You can now say to students, "Try this color today as you write," or "Kate, please make sure to get to the purple color today." When students come up to you and say, "I'm done now", you can reference a color for them to go back to their seats and try.

Draw it

Write the first sound

Write the last sound

Write the whole word

Write a sentence

Write 2 sentences

Write 4 sentences

Write a paragraph

WOW (web, organize, write)

Some topics we have used at this center are:

A person who lived in Colonial times
A person aboard the Santa Maria
The principal
A seed
A specific animal
The sun
A solid
A character from a story
The list is endless.

Below are some examples.

Pretend you were a seed.

I am a Lima Been. The first thing I do is staert out us'a Lima Been. Than I steart To Grow The roots, And Than I Steart to grow a stem. And Than I steart To Grow Leaves, Than I steort To work on my flower's. And They make new Lima Beens And I need sun, And I need food And I nee soils And I need A litul Dirt. I hav roots That hold me down To The Girond. I'm cold But it is Osum undur The Grownd. I Live in The Growind whith my Dold And my mom And my littel Brawhur The Persun That plentid me is Blair

Tyler

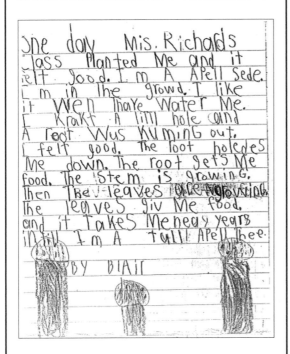

One day Mis. Richards class Planted me and it felt good. I'm A Apell sede. I'm in the growd. I like it wen thare water me. I Krakt A littl hole and A root wus Kuming out. I felt good. The Loot holedes me down. The root gets me food. The stem is growing. Then The leaves are growing. The leaves giv me food. and it Takes me neay years intill I'm A tall Apell Thee.

BY BLAIT

What do you want to be when you grow up? Pretend you were a _____.

ITZBAPR

(I want to be a power ranger.)

I'm going to be a spase Pilot when I grow up. I want to be a spase Pilit. Becau- se I thik it will. Be fun. I'm going to start out as a Person Who rides in the back. And when I get older I will ride in the frunt. And when I get to Be a mother I will drive The Plan. And it will Be fun.

What do you think about the bunny? (This assignment was given after reading the book *The Little Rabbit Who Wanted Red Wings* by Carolyn Sherwin Bailey.

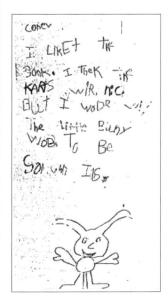

I liked the book. I think the characters were nice. But I wonder why the little bunny wanted to be someone else.

If I were that bunny I would have learned a lesson about I'm a good person. I don't have to be another person.

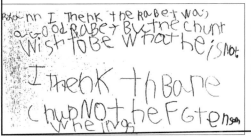

I think the rabbit was a good rabbit. But he shouldn't wish to be what he is not. I think the bunny should not have gotten some wings.

What do think about the Easter bunny?

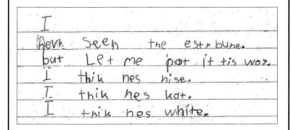

I never seen the Easter bunny but let me put it this way. I think he's nice. I think he's cute. I think he's white.

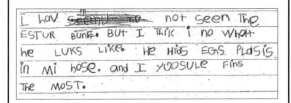

I have not seen the Easter bunny. But I think I know what he looks like. He hide eggs places in my house and I usually find the most.

Reading Center/ Classroom Library Posters

The ultimate goal at the reading center is for students to read and comprehend. There are often three types of students at the classroom library or reading center.

One:

Some students do a beautiful job at the reading center. They choose an appropriate text, settle into silent reading, and read for meaning.

Two:

Some students do an acceptable job at the reading center. They may be struggling readers or readers that do not have great comprehension. They are not fluent but they are exhibiting some positive reading strategies. For example, they are attentive to pictures and print, have a literal, basic comprehension of what they read, and can attend to the reading task.

Three:

There are also students that have no attention span and struggle with the reading. These are students who grab a handful of books, "read" them in two seconds and then yell over at you that they are done. They may start "fooling around" because their attention span with books is over. These students are "flippers." Their idea of reading is to flip or fan through the book and that's it.

Students who like reading will read for meaning. They have the attention span to work with a book and use the reading center as a "typical library." They get a book and get to work. That's great. However, you need to have something available for those students who are inattentive to print and pictures, flip through books, and are movers and doers. That's where Library Posters come in. Have six "mini posters" hanging in the center at all times, although all six may not always be used.

Take six pieces of 12x18 construction paper and laminate them. Hang them up in your classroom library. Once you hang them up, you'll never have to take them down again. Use visa vise marks or dry erase and then all you have to do is erase the old info and put up the new. Let's look at what is on the mini posters.

Remember, the ultimate goal here is just pure reading. These poster activities are for students who need more focus and hands-on, manipulative activities with text. Your great readers will probably not work with these posters. They just want to read.

Each poster has a different focus. You want students to find these things in their books and highlight them (page 36 explains and shows highlighting tape). Some of these ideas are better for emergent readers, some are better for developing readers, and some for students who just need to move and manipulate something. You'll choose whichever and how many posters suit the needs of your students. Posters change depending on how long you spend with the specific curriculum and information.

Colors

There is a "scribble" of a color along with the color word written on the poster. Students must look at the pictures and find that color on the page. Every time they find something that color, they must highlight it with highlighting tape. This has been a great activity for language development. As students are looking at the pictures, they are talking to themselves about what they see in the pictures. You will learn a lot just by listening in and watching students do this. It is also quite entertaining.

The highlighting color was pink one week. The following is a conversation I listened in on while Richard was highlighting:

"There's a pink dress the mom has on. The dad doesn't have any pink on cause it's a girl color. Look, there is a pink stripe on her hat. There's no pink in the garden. I wonder why the pumpkin is so big? Hey, look! They turned the pumpkin into a crib for the baby. The baby has a pink blanket. I never had a pink blanket. I had a little bear I always slept with."

Wow! This is a child who usually does a picture walk in two seconds. He flips. He's done. All of this conversation was said for just three pages! The highlighting slowed him down so he could literally attend to the pictures. Notice the connections, opinions, and questions that went on in just three pages. This has been an incredible activity for my emergent readers and struggling learners.

Letters

There is a letter written on the poster. Students must look at the pictures and find things that begin with that letter. Students could also find words that contain that letter. This is a nice follow-up to letters and sounds that are being focused on during whole-group instruction. This poster also works well if you have a classroom with many beginning or developing readers, and only a handful of ones that still need work with letters and sounds. This poster is a "must do" for those students. It would be a follow-up to what was being worked on in small flexible groups with the teacher.

Spelling and Phonics

Whatever your focus is in this area, that is what is written on the poster. You could color code this poster to differentiate for different levels. I often have something written in red, something in blue, and something in green. I write the grade level curriculum in red. Red tells me that is the "hot" stuff, usually the whole-group instruction at grade level. Another color is an easier task and the last is a challenging task.

Sight words

Whatever sight words are being focused on are written on the poster. This could also be differentiated with three colors as described above.

Story Elements

The story element changes on this poster. For example: characters, setting, problem/solution, and resolution. This poster naturally differentiates itself based on the books students are reading.

Emergent students are finding the story elements in the pictures.

Developing readers are finding the elements in both the pictures and text.

Students reading novels are finding them in the text. With "novel readers," you can have them work with textual support as well as scanning and skimming for information. Also, inferential items come up frequently.

For example, when "characters" is written on the chart, students have to find text that backs up an opinion of the character. How do we know about the characters? We know about them by:

what they say,
what they do,
what others think about them,
what others say about them,
what they, themselves, are thinking.

Language Arts Skills

Anything you are teaching can go on this chart. Some examples are parts of speech, compound words, plurals, possessives, and punctuation marks.

Literary Elements:

Some examples are flashbacks, similes, metaphors, author's purpose, theme, and conflict. Whatever you are teaching can go on this chart.

You could have different posters for different students to focus upon. You could have a poster for each needs-based group or guided reading group. This is really an open-ended activity for your classroom library/reading center.

Wikki Stix can be used instead of highlighting tape. The Wikki Stixs are organized the same way as the tape.

These posters are not strategies. They are meant to give students specific things to look for in their books. Classrooms should have many reading strategy posters available throughout the room for students. For example: What do I do when I get stuck on a word? How do I monitor my reading? What connections have I made?

Wordless Books

Wordless books are books that contain illustrations but no text. There is a bibliography of wordless books on the following page.

Why Wordless Books?

These books give students opportunities to use their imaginations and create their own stories using the pictures as prompts.

You'll never hear "I have nothing to write about." With wordless books, one of the hardest parts of writing is already done. The topic is organized and well developed. All students have to do is write what they see. There is no more struggling with ideas and topics for writing.

Wordless books help build the foundations of language. Students verbalize the actions and details on each page.

These are great resources for second language learners or ESL classrooms. They stimulate students' imaginations and develop reading and writing skills.

Any ability level can be successful with these books. Younger children and struggling learners may label pictures using stickies or write one sentence about each page on lined paper. Older and more fluent writers can work on their development of story and plot.

Basic story structure is modeled in these books: character, setting, problem, solution, events, etc. They help children understand comprehension of story language and story patterns.

Students practice their oral speaking by becoming storytellers and "reading" the book to an audience.

Students might not write about the whole book page by page, but sometimes one page sparks an idea and students will use that as a springboard for writing.

Activities and Ideas

After students have written stories about a wordless book, work with comparing and contrasting the different stories. Graph similarities and differences. Use Venn diagrams.

Make a class story. Each child writes one page of the story.

Use wordless books as your topic for interactive writing. Students can dictate and the teacher writes.

Instructional Strategies and Skills

Teachers can incorporate many skills, strategies, and mini-lesson topics into students' writing. Because the wordless book has the story line already complete, students can put their efforts into applying and utilizing the skills and strategies into their writing. Some topics we've used are:

Descriptive words
Using adjectives and adverbs
Using dialogue
Using words other than "said"
Using complete sentences
Character descriptions
Setting description
Opening lines
Editing
Revising
Sequencing of events
Story development
Main idea, supporting detail
Similes
Metaphors
The list is endless.

My students love wordless books for so many reasons. They have so much success as readers and writers and speakers. Their confidence level is amazing.

Below is a bibliography of wordless books.

Alphabet City
    by Stephen Johnson
A Boy, A Dog, and A Friend
    by Mercer Mayer
A Boy, A Dog, and A Frog
    by Mercer Mayer
Deep in the Forest
    by Brinton Turkle
Flotsam
    by David Wiesner
Frog on His Own
    by Mercer Mayer
Frog, Where Are You
    by Mercer Mayer
Looking Down
    by Steve Jenkins
Oops
    by Arthur Geisert
The Red Book
    by Barbara Lehman
You Can't Take a Balloon Into the Museum of Fine Arts
    by Jacqueline Preiss Weitzman & Robin Preiss Glasser
You Can't Take a Balloon Into the Metropolitan Museum
    by Jacqueline Preiss Weitzman & Robin Preiss Glasser
Will's Mammoth
    by Rafe Martin
Zoom
    by Istvan Banyai

Most of the wordless books are available at www.huskytrailpress.com

This sample is from a second grader writing about the pictures in the book *Flotsam*.

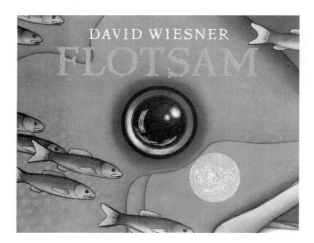

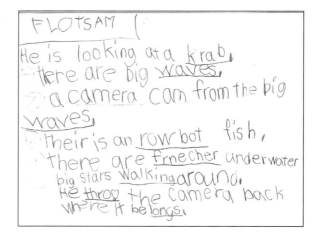

FLOTSAM (
He is looking at a krab,
there are big waves,
a camera cam from the big
waves,
their is an rowbot fish,
there are frnecher underwater
big stars walking around,
He throo the camera back
where it belongs.

This sample is from a second grader writing about the pictures in the book *The Red Book*.

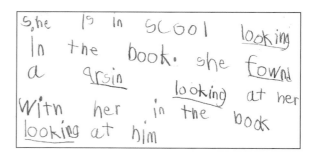

She is going to scool,
She is working,
She found a red book.
She is runing,
She is in scool,
She is looking in the book.
She found a mug in the
red book,
he fand a red book too.
he looket in the book.

She is in scool looking
in the book. she fownd
a grsin looking at her
witn her in the book
looking at him

Editing and Revising

You may be thinking, "How does editing and revising fit into the assignment section of this book?" Students should edit and revise every text they write. Not that they have to rewrite a final copy and make their papers picture perfect; but proofreading should be addressed on a daily basis. So the bigger questions become, "How can you differentiate editing and revising? Do you have to meet with each child one on one? Do you just correct their mistakes and hand back the papers? Students are all at different levels in their writing abilities, so what do you do?"

Children cannot be good editors and revisers if they aren't reading through their papers at least once. They must be proofreaders in order to be competent at editing and revising. So step one is to get students to reread their papers, not to make corrections, but just get into the habit of rereading!

At the bottom of their papers, write down some misspelled words. Don't try to list all the problems. You will have students whose papers have every single word misspelled and to ask them to fix everything is too much. Remember the first step is to get them to just reread their papers. The more capable students are, the more words you write at the bottom of their papers for them to correct. The less capable students are, the fewer words they are asked to correct.

Students "wave through" the misspelled words and write the correct spelling above. The goal is that all students proofread their papers and make corrections. The numbers of corrections are based on their abilities. As students become more capable through growth and practice, instead of writing the word correctly at the bottom of their papers, start to turn their attention to your word walls. You might write "ww" three times at the bottom of their papers. That means there are three words that need to be corrected and they can be found on the word wall.

Below is an example

Character Fun

This is one of my students' favorite assignments. Each week or every other week, they get a character from a book they are reading. The character is cut out and glued onto a piece of construction paper. Students have to turn that character into a picture and write about it. There are four options for the assigned writing.

Write a new ending.
Write a new chapter that takes place somewhere in the middle of the story.
Write a retelling of the story.
Write a creative piece that has nothing to do with the story.

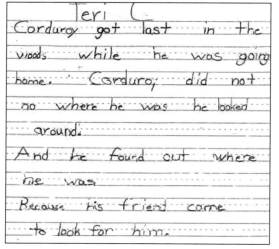

Teri C
Corduroy got last in the woods while he was going home. Corduroy did not no where he was he looked around. And he found out where he was Because his friend came to look for him.

Matthew
one day Cordroe watt ro tvie wads he gow a gost it skadd nam na giv tdnb waps sa ne hd in the tel he saw a nagse wa tne gast wat in the hae nesnakdan afs geska

This center was really an eye opener for me. Sometimes on the surface, students look like they are doing fine, but when we really dig into their work, we find they are not as strong as we thought. Let's look at the examples on page 110 from the book *Corduroy*. The direction for this assignment was "free choice." Students could choose any of the four options they want. The left sample is from a child named Teri. She is a first grader who "missed the cut off date" because of her birthday, so is an older first grader. The child whose paper is on the right is Matthew. Matthew just made the cut off date, so he is a very young first grader.

At first glance the paper on the left "looks" much more proficient. You can understand the picture. It is very neat. You can read her writing and her spelling is good. The paper on the right has a picture that is full of items that can't all be identified. It has a lot of "scribbling" on it. Corduroy looks like he is floating in the air above some kind of monster. The writing is very difficult to read and there are many spelling errors. My immediate response, and that of many colleagues, is that we are more concerned about Matthew than Teri.

Now let's dig deeper.

Here is Teri's written response:

Corduroy got lost in the woods while he was going home. Corduroy did not know where he was. He looked around.

That is what Teri turned in the first time. It is exactly what happened in the book. Her spelling is great because she had the book on her desk and was looking for the words to spell. Teri will not write anything

unless she knows how to spell it. I put two stickies on her paper. One asked, "Does he ever find out where he is?" The other asked, "How does he ever get home." She literally answered each question. She wrote:

And he found out where he was. Because his friend came to look for him.

Teri is a very literal learner. She is not a risk taker. She wrote exactly what happened in the book.

Now let's look at Matt's.

One day Corduroy went into the woods. He saw a ghost. It scared him. He saw two wolves so he hid in the tree. He saw a house. When the ghost went in the house he snuck down and escaped.

Look at Matt's picture now. Corduroy is up in the tree. The "scribbles" are the leaves of the tree. The ghost is under him saying, "BOO." The two wolves are there and so is the house.

Who are you more concerned about now? Our concern is Teri, who is really a full year older than Matt. On the surface, Teri "looks" great. Her pictures are clear. We can read her writing. It's neat and her spelling is good. Teri is always in her seat doing what is asked of her. Matt, on the other hand, "looks" like he might be having difficulties. His picture is hard to understand. His writing is not neat and very difficult to read. He's all over the place in the classroom, never in his seat. These are two very different children in the same classroom.

Usually with younger children in first and second grade, the characters from books change every week. Their books are shorter and stories last about a week or are read in a day or two.

With older students, grades three and four, there are two ideas that work with this activity. Characters may change although the story stays the same for a couple of weeks. For example, we were reading James and the Giant Peach in fourth grade, so each week I added another character from the book to this center. Another idea is to use short children's literature and concentrate on a specific skill modeled in that book for students to use in their writing. Below are fourth grade examples completed after reading the children's book *Foodle*, by Pat Pavelka. The book concentrates on adjectives, so notice the adjectives in their writing.

Here are extension ideas for Character Fun. These extension ideas came from my students. Each time the character was changed, I took away the old one and put out the new one. My students complained about this and wanted to keep the old characters out and available to use. I said, "No." My thought was they had used that character last week. We were on to a new book or chapter and I wanted them to use another character. Here's what they wanted to do. My third graders wanted Encyclopedia Brown to meet Cam Jansen and talk about the cases they were working on! First graders wanted Frog and Toad to meet Emily Elizabeth and Clifford and talk about best friends.

You can also connect science and social studies to this activity. Have pictures available for students to use that coordinate with your content area topic. When we were working with the farm, I had pictures of farm animals, a barn, a tractor, and a farmer. When were working with the ocean, I had pictures of sea animals, a ship, a boat, and shells. Students put their character into a scene that was tied to our curriculum.

Ideas, connections, and implementation strategies.

Ideas, connections, and implementation strategies.

Chapter

Ongoing Assessment Window

Preface

When I used to hear the word "assessment," the hairs on the back of my neck stood up. I'd think of getting ready for my traditional Friday tests.

> Making up tests at home.
> Running papers off in the teacher's room, when there were two colleagues in front of me and the buses were arriving ***now.***
> Knowing certain students would say they were done in two minutes and had not even tried.
> Knowing the test would be too easy for some students and too hard for others.
> Spending hours grading papers since assessment was only a paper/pencil task.

I saw assessment as the end product. Assessment was done when teaching a concept was finished and that was that. I never saw assessment as driving my instruction. Instead it was seen as a completion of my instruction.

My idea of assessment has changed greatly. We now know that assessment should truly drive instruction. If assessment drives instruction, then we need to assess before and during, not just after.

The visual below follows the cyclical path of assessment, evaluation, and instruction. It is a continuous process that never ends.

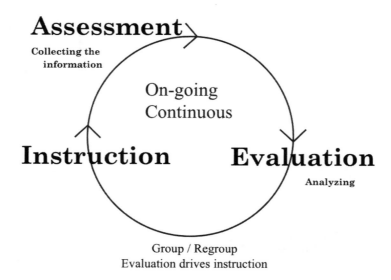

Assessment is the collecting and gathering of information.
Evaluation is the analyzing and making judgments about the assessment.
Instruction is driven by the above two items.

Where does grading come in? Grading is the reporting system. Grading really should not come in until you and your students have gone through this cycle at least twice. Students need a significant amount of time to practice before the actual grading takes place.

I think of the time I was learning how to drive a stick shift. I got to a red light where the road was on a bit of an incline, not a hill, but just a little incline. The light changed three times before I could get through it! When it would turn green, I couldn't coordinate the shift pedal with my left foot, the gas pedal with my right foot, and the actual shift with my right hand. I stalled the car, raced the engine and went nowhere, jerked the car up a foot, and then stopped. Had I been graded while learning, I would have achieved an "F." I needed a lot of assessment, evaluation, and then instruction before a grade would have had any meaning.

Think of a time when you were learning something: playing a sport, knitting, cooking, building something, painting, etc. You probably needed practice time before you wanted anyone to grade your achievements.

There is a place in assessment programs for the traditional paper/pencil tasks, such as tests from publishers and teacher-made quizzes and tests. A good assessment program includes a variety of classroom assessments. You want assessment to be ongoing. Teacher observation is at the center of ongoing assessment and evaluation. It means that you are constantly collecting and gathering information. You are then using that information to form flexible groups and follow-up assignments. You're looking for improvement and increasing achievement.

In this chapter you'll find ways to collect information before, during, and after teaching. Many of the ideas will refer you back to an activity in one of the other Windows of Opportunity.

Ongoing Assessment, here we go.

Traffic Lights

This is a type of formative assessment that can be used in any subject area. It works well in both whole group and small flexible group settings. This will let you monitor all students instead of just one student who is answering a question and talking. Students need a blank traffic light paper (see reproducible page 155). They will cut out three circles: one red, one green, and one yellow. The three colored circles will fit on top of the three noncolored circles on the traffic light.

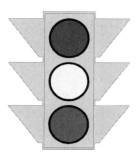

You can use this activity a number of different ways. Use the traffic light when asking a specific question to your whole class or small group. Students will place a colored circle on their traffic lights that indicate their knowledge of the question asked.

Red means, "I do not know the answer."
Yellow means, "I think I know the answer but I'm not quite sure."
Green means, "I have it. I know the answer."
You can also use this activity as a

preassessment to a unit or curriculum that is going to be taught. For example, if you have a unit on landforms, ask your students how they feel about their knowledge of landforms.

Red means, "I do not have any understanding or prior knowledge of landforms."
Yellow means, " I think I have an idea of what landforms are. I have a little knowledge.
Green means, "I understand and know a lot about landforms.

Completely on their own, my students decided that this traffic light activity would be good to use in their 3T Clubs. See page 75 for information on 3T Clubs. When the two "teachers" of the 3T Clubs work with the third member, they ask the third member to use the traffic light to show them how his/her understanding is going.

White Boards

This is another type of formative assessment that can be used in any subject area. It works well in both whole group and small flexible group settings. Students need a white board and dry erase marker.

Ask your students a question. Instead of one student raising a hand and answering the question, everyone must answer the question on his or her white board. This allows you to monitor and give immediate feedback to students. Students are always praised for trying. You want to make sure this does not turn into a competition between students.

If a student does not know or is not sure of the answer, there are some options available.

Option One
The child puts a question mark on his whiteboard. When we start discussing the answer, I say to my class, "If you have written a question mark, listen carefully to the answer. I'll be calling on you to repeat the answer."

Option Two
The child writes an answer and puts a question mark next to it. Depending upon the student, you may call on that student to share his or her answer and then discuss whether or not it is correct. Also discuss why that child wrote that response.

If you have students that would not like to be put on the spot, do not call on someone with a question mark next to his/her answer. After the correct answer is given, all students rewrite the correct answer on their boards. Then call on a child that had the question mark to repeat the correct answer.

Prove It!

This is a great assessment piece for inferencing, drawing conclusions, and using textual support. It works well with both whole group and small flexible group settings. Before using this activity, review the details about highlighting tape on page 36.

> What it looks like
> How students use it
> How to organize it on cards for students
> Making grab tabs, etc.

Begin modeling and working with literal questions. This will teach students the process and will give them success right away. I'll use *Goldilocks and the Three Bears* for an example. Ask students a literal question such as, "What is the name of the girl that went to the bear's house?" They usually all yell, "Goldilocks!" Then ask students to prove it. Have them find the answer in their books and highlight it. Ask another easy literal question such as, "How many bears were there in the story?" Students usually all remark that I'm asking such easy questions. They all yell, "Three. That's so easy!" Then ask them to prove it. Have them find the answer in their books and highlight it. Follow this process for a number of easy questions. You may find that you will use this easy format for a week before you begin to shift to more complex, inferential questions.

One of the skills that we are subtly working on here is scanning and skimming for information. Scanning and skimming is a difficult task to teach, especially for young children. I am amazed at how fast students catch on to this. Also rereading the text is helping some students with their fluency development.

After working with literal questions for a while, it's time to switch to comprehension questions that are not literal. Give students questions where they must infer and draw conclusions. These are the most difficult questions for students to answer. Most students look for the answers to be right there and touchable, like the literal questions. Let's use the book *Goldilocks and the Three Bears* again for our example. Usually on the last page of the book, Goldilocks wakes up and sees the bears. The text may read something like this:

Goldilocks saw the bears. She screamed and her hair stood up. She ran out the door as fast as she could. She said, "I'm never going back there again."

The question I ask students is, "How does Goldilocks feel?" The students all say either scared or afraid. I tell them they are correct. They are asked to go back in the book and prove it, like we've previously been doing. They are so funny. They read the page and say, "The answer is not there." So I tell them they must have the wrong answer. Goldilocks must not be scared. They all start arguing that they have the correct answer, "She is scared." I ask them again to prove it, to find the answer in their books and highlight it. It is so entertaining to watch them. They read the page once more and yell out again, with more annoyance in their tone, "The answer is not there." Even my proficient readers will behave this way.

Now we start the teaching. Ask students how they know that Goldilocks was scared. We will discuss the text where it says:

She screamed and her hair stood up. She ran out the door as fast as she could. She said, "I'm never going back there again."

Students are asked to highlight those sentences because they led to the answer. The answer was not right there in those words, but those words led to the answer. Many times now, when students are given questions that require them to draw conclusions and make inferences, they do not write the answers. Instead, they find textual support that leads them to an answer or prediction.

Assessment Grids

You want daily, ongoing assessments to be quick and easy. Otherwise they become too cumbersome and are not used, or if they are used, the data is not analyzed and used to drive instruction. Assessment grids are one of my favorite formative assessments. You use formative assessments, like the grids we will be discussing, to determine where students are in their understanding of curriculum. You then use that data to adjust your instruction.

Assessment grids can be used during most of the activities in the four Windows of Opportunity: Student Engagement, Questioning, Flexible Grouping and Assignments. Grids can also be used in different curriculum areas. You'll find two grids in the reproducible section on pages 156 and 157.

I never thought I could assess many individual students while working with my whole class. Usually I would instruct the class for a period of time, and then give students some kind of follow-up activity to do. I never thought that part of my instruction time should be spent assessing as students were in the midst of learning. My process used to be teaching until I disseminated all the information that was planned for that period, and then assign something.

Instruction now looks like this:

Teach a bit, assess, teach some more, assess what they've learned so far, teach again, and assess again. This is a process where teaching and assessing go hand in hand, in small chunks together, rather than two separate, isolated processes.

Sometimes the information you receive on the grid will be more preassessment data. You'll see where individual students are in regard to their understanding of new concepts and curriculum being taught. You'll learn what you need to reteach and what small flexible groups you might need to make. Sometimes the information you receive is at the end of a unit or curriculum. Your data from the grids will be more summative in nature than formative.

Grids have allowed me to change to the process of teaching and assessing going hand in hand. The top of the grid has a blank line for you to put whatever curriculum you are assessing. Students' names are written down the left side of the grid. The grid has ten boxes across. Each box is worth ten points. You can get a traditional percentage grade if you need. I use checks and minuses. If there are three minuses across Kate's row, then her grade is 70%. If Chen has two minuses across his row, his grade is 80%. If Laura has four minuses across her row, her grade is 60%.

Week(s) of _____										Curriculum _____	
Name											
Kate	✓	✓	—	✓	—	—	✓	✓	✓	✓	70%
Chen	✓	✓	—	✓	✓	✓	✓	—	✓	✓	80%
Laura	—	✓	✓	—	✓	—	—	✓	✓	✓	60%

We'll look at two different examples: a reading lesson using a piece of literature with first graders and a lesson on nouns with third graders.

Using the grids with a first grade piece of literature

The whole class has a copy of the story titled, *The Adventures of Victor* by Pat Pavelka. Pages one through seven of the book talk about a cat named Victor who is moving to the city. After they have read pages one through seven, you may be ready to stop and assess how students are comprehending. Have students partner up (see page 27 for partnering ideas) and talk for three to five minutes about what has happened so far in the story. You may ask specific questions for them to discuss. As students are discussing with their partners, walk around the room with your grid.

Keep the grids on a clipboard. Stop at different students and ask them a question or questions relating to the story. Put a check if their answers were correct or a minus if they were confused. You may ask a student only one question or you may ask several questions. Each answer given gets a check or minus on the grid. You can usually get to half of your students during their discussing and processing. Many times you'll hear the same misinformation and know you must reteach a concept or review something that happened in the book.

Come back together as a class and have a discussion about what has happened so far. Correct misunderstandings that you heard while assessing. Then continue this process. Read from pages eight through eleven. Ask students to partner up again and talk for three to five minutes about what has happened in the story. You may ask specific questions for them to discuss. As students are discussing with their partners, again walk around the room with your grid.

One of the grids I use a lot when working with literature is titled Connections (see pages 54–60 for connection ideas). In the grid boxes I put TS (text-to-self), TT (text-to-text), or TW (text-to-world), along with a check or minus. The check means the student gave a good, thought-provoking connection. The minus means the child gave a literal, not deep connection or no connection at all.

You will see lots of trends with your grids. For example, in the grid below, all of the TW connections have minuses. I know I must reteach and work on this concept some more. The grid below shows only three children. When you look at your whole class you will see whether you need to reteach and practice with the whole class or with just a small needs-based group.

Week(s) of _____				Connections				
Name								
Kate	TS✓	TS✓	TT✓	TW_	TS✓	TS✓		
Chen	TW–	TW–	TS✓	TS✓	TT✓			
Laura	TW–	TS✓	TS–	TT_	TW–			

Using the grids with a lesson on nouns with third graders.

Let's say you introduced the concept of nouns to your class. Ask them to now partner up and discuss their knowledge of nouns. While they are discussing, walk around the room with the grid on a clipboard. Listen in on their conversations. Put a check or a minus in students' boxes depending upon what you hear. You could just visit students and ask them to give you examples of nouns. Mark their responses on the grid.

Now come back together. Teach again, practice some more and repeat the same step as above: students discuss while you walk around and assess with the grid. Come back together again. Reteach, give more examples, and address all the misunderstandings you heard while walking around the room.

Ask students to get a piece of paper and list as many nouns as they can in three minutes. You walk around with the grid again. This time there is no discussion. What you usually will see at this point is that students who had minuses to begin with are starting to get checks. They have had multiple opportunities to process the information and practice orally with peers and with you.

Preassessment

You'll need to gather preassessment information before you start your instruction. The information you receive will affect your instruction in a number of different ways.

> Adjustment for students who have already mastered the content.
>
> Support for those who will need many opportunities to practice and apply the content.
>
> Practice for students who have some of the content understood but need a little more engagement with it.

There are two reproducibles on pages 158 and 159 that can be used for preassessment in virtually any curriculum area.

Below is an example using the reproducible on page 159 with a second grade science unit on plants.

12 southeast states	tributaries, Mississippi River, river basin, mouth
What do you know about...?	
agriculture, growing season, cash crop, irrigation	coal, labor union, miners

Above is an example using the reproducible on page 158 with a fourth grade social studies unit on the Southeast.

What do you know about...?

living things and nonliving things	plants	parts of a plant
products from plants and trees	photosynthesis	what do plants need?

Anecdotal Records for Reading

Informal running records are very manageable and can easily be integrated into your daily instruction and routines. These often provide rich, anecdotal information for you to use in planning for literacy instruction. I recommend using a three ring binder with number dividers. See the picture below.

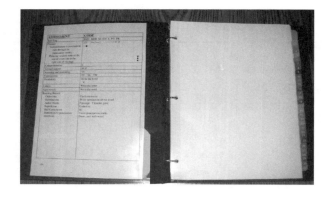

Each child is given a number and has that section in your notebook where you will write your observations. There are no forms or run-offs needed. Use blank pieces of paper, lined or unlined. These assessments can be done during SSR time or while working with a guided reading group.

Do not feel you have to have your notebook look exactly the way mine looks. Take these ideas and make them fit your specific needs. You do not want to do a lot of writing because that will take too long to do and it will also take too long to read through. You want this to be

quick and easy, yet give you specific data with which to organize your instruction. Basically, you ask the child a question or listen to his or her reading. Write down a code that represents what you heard or asked. If the child answered correctly or did a good job with the reading, that's all you do. Leave the code alone. If the child answered incorrectly or had a problem with something in the reading, then draw a line through the code you wrote. Below are the areas I assess and the codes I use.

Retelling

I ask the child to give a retelling of what was just read. If I write "BME" it means the child gave a good retelling that included the beginning, middle and end. If I draw a line through "~~BME~~" it means the child could not give a retelling.

Sometimes a child will give a retelling but it is all out of order. The information is there but not sequenced correctly. For this I write MEB (middle, end, beginning). It tells me the student had some of the information from the story but needs work with sequencing.

There are other notations you may want to make during a retelling.

"SL" means the student gave specific story language from the book. ~~SL~~ with a line through it means the child did not use any story language or vocabulary from the story. For example, when assessing a retelling of *The Wild Things*, Jeremiah said, "And Max traveled over a day and night to where the wild things were. And they roared their terrible roars, and they gnashed their terrible teeth." I wrote "SL" on the page in Jeremiah's section of the notebook. He used direct story language and vocabulary from that story. Maria said, "This kid went over the water and met some big dinosaurs. " I wrote ~~SL~~ with the line through it because she had no story language or vocabulary from the book.

"CH" means they included a lot of detail and information about the character. "S" means they included a lot of detail and information about the setting. "P/S" means they included detail about a problem and solution. "PR" means they made a prediction. If students left any of these out of their retelling, I put the code with a line through it.

I used to think I had to write down everything the student said when retelling. It became a daunting task so I did not assess retelling as much as I should have. You may find you have students who are having difficulty with retelling. You want to take those students in small flexible groups or pair options and have them practice retelling daily. This anecdotal assessment is quick and will give you very specific information as to how they are developing in their ability to retell.

Fluency

You can write three things to note students' fluency.

/ / / /   Put some lines on the paper. This tells you the child is reading word by word.

/-/-/-/-/-   This tells you the child is beginning to read in phrases. He is not a word by word reader, but not yet fluent.

———→ F   This tells you the child is a fluent reader.

•
•
•   If the child stops at the right side of every line on the page, whether there is a period there or not, write three dots on the right side of the piece of notebook paper.

——•——   The dot in the middle of the line means that as the child reads, he or she runs through the periods. The child doesn't stop.

Comprehension

When asking a comprehension question, write a "C." If the child gives a correct answer, just leave the "C." If the child can not give a correct response, then put a line through the "~~C.~~" You can open your notebook and see right away who is having comprehension issues because all of the "Cs" have lines through them. Sometimes you might see the following:

———→ F   ~~C~~   ~~C~~   ~~C~~   ~~C~~

This means the child is reading fluently. He or she sounds great, but four comprehension questions were asked and the child could not answer any of them. You may want to note what kinds of questions you are asking. For example, are you asking literal questions or questions that lead to inferencing and drawing conclusions? Some students do very well with literal, right there questions. When given thought provoking and critical thinking kinds of questions, their achievement goes down. You could note that with a "C-L" (literal question) or a "C-D" (question that needs the student to draw conclusions.) There are limitless ways to work with comprehension coding. Choose exactly what you are looking for in regard to comprehension and then make a code for your notations.

Textual Support

Many times when asking questions, you want the students to be able to go back into the text and prove their answers. "SUP" means they were able to go back and find textual support to back up an answer. "SUP" with a line through it means they could not support an answer with textual support. You may want to note what kind of answer the child is looking for: a literal, a think and search, or an evaluative kind.

Scanning and Skimming

This is a difficult concept to teach. The only way students get better at scanning and skimming is to do it; to practice it on a daily basis. One way to help students with this is to ask them to go back into the book for textual support. Watch what they do. Are they able to scan and skim? Usually students do one of two things: read too slowly or too quickly. They reread the whole text again slowly, word-by-word, as if reading it for the first time. Or they take two seconds and say, "I'm done. I can't find it." "SS" means they did a good job of scanning and skimming. "SS" with a line through it means they were not able to scan and skim.

Connections

"TS" stands for text-to-self connections.
"TT" stands for text-to-text connections.
"TW" stands for text-to-world connections.

Ask students to make connections. Depending upon what kind of connection you asked for, you will write the above code. If they cannot make a connection, then draw a line through the code. You might also want to note the degree to which the connection was made. Was it a high level, critical thinking connection or a surface level, literal one?

Vocabulary

You want to note whether students skip over words they do not know or stop to ponder the meaning of a new word. This is not the same as decoding, where you are looking for pronunciation of the word. Here you are looking for understanding of the word's meaning. There are two options that you can use. Sometimes you'll just write "V". Other times write the word. For example, if the word was "blustery" and the child read it correctly and gave the correct meaning, you would write "blustery" on the page in the notebook. If the child did not know the meaning of the word, then you would write "blustery" with a line through it.

Letters and Sounds

Sometimes you want to know what letters and sounds a child knows or is having difficulty with. Just write the letter and either leave it as is or put a line through it.

Sight Words

Sometimes you want to know what sight words a child knows or is having difficulty with. Write the word and either leave it as is or put a line through it.

There are the traditional running record codes and symbols that include assessing the following reading behaviors: omissions, substitutions, aided words, repetitions, self-corrections, and insertions.

You want to set up a notebook tailored to your needs and the needs of your students. Your notebook will be an invaluable aid for you to know the following information:
   students' strengths,
   students' weaknesses,
   what to teach,
   what needs to be retaught and practiced,
   how to form small flexible groups,
   which students need to be challenged,
   which students need to be supported.

There is a reproducible on page 160 that has the codes summarized. This reproducible is the first page of an anecdotal notebook. It helps remind you of what kinds of behaviors and strategies you should be looking for.

Comprehension

Traditional assessment in comprehension usually involved giving students questions to answer, correcting those answers, and then getting a grade. Following are alternatives to assessing children's comprehension of texts.

Marking and Posting

Instead of writing the answers to questions, students mark and post the answers with stickies, highlight tape, or Wikki Stixs. A question students were given was, "Using both the text and pictures, prove that Victor's new home in the country was different than his home in the city." Below is what one child posted.

Another way to work with marking and posting is just to have the students put a sticky on the page where the answer can be found. Students were given four questions. They put the corresponding number on the page or pages where the answer was found. See the example below.

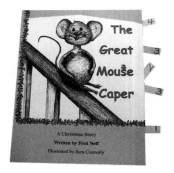

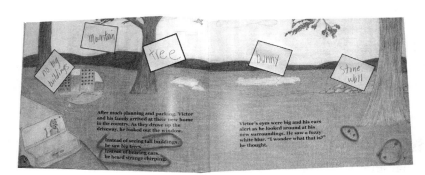

In the example above, going from left to right the stickies say: no big buildings, mountain, tree, bunny, stone wall. The child used Wikki Stixs to circle the text stating that the character saw trees instead of tall buildings, and strange chirping instead of cars. He also circled the flowers on the right page.

Graphic Organizers

Ask students to visualize and draw what they read. Depending upon students' grade levels and abilities, they might draw a graphic organizer about a chapter or about the whole book. There are many graphic organizer forms available. However, I find if I give students blank paper, I learn a lot more about their comprehension than if they were to fill in a form.

Following are two graphic organizers from chapter eight of the book *Elmer and the Dragon* by Ruth Stiles Gannett. I numbered the graphic organizers so it would be easier to explain what each child drew. A child who is working below grade level completed the first example. A child working a little above grade level completed the second example.

1. They are digging for buried treasure.
2. They found the buried treasure and took it out of the ground.
3. It was locked.
4. There was a note in it.
5. They had a celebration.

This is a very literal recall of the chapter. There is also incorrect information. Numbers one and two have a boy digging for the treasure. The dragon actually got the treasure. Number three shows that the child knows the treasure is locked, but he does not show who got the key and unlocked it. Number four shows that a note was in the buried treasure. There was also gold, a gold watch and chain, and a sterling silver harmonica which this child did not show. Number five shows the celebration the characters had with a tangerine on each plate.

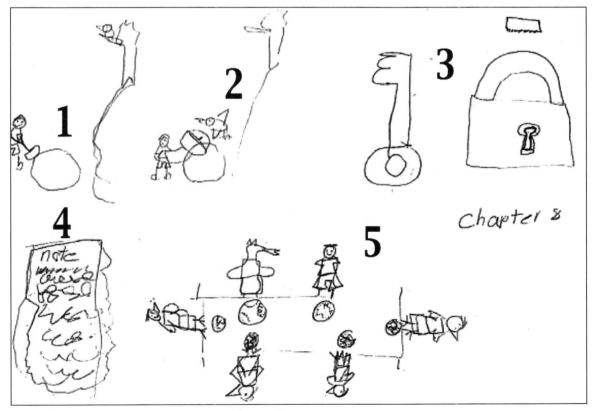

Example one

Example two

Flipbooks

Flipbooks are great organizers for students when they are given questions from which they must draw conclusions and make inferences. Take a piece of lined paper and fold it in half. Cut the top into as many flaps as there are questions. On the outside flaps write down the page number or numbers where the information is located that will help students answer the questions.

Many times in my small flexible group setting, I will have students organize their flipbooks so when they go back to their seats they have a reference for help. See the example below.

1. The dragon was looking at the buried treasure and helped get it out.
2. The treasure was locked.
3. The bird got the key.
4. Elmer took the note out of the treasure box.
5. Elmer organized for the celebration by setting the table with tangerines, pewter plates, skunk cabbage and ostrich ferns.
6. In the treasure was a sterling silver harmonica that Elmer was given. When he played it all the canaries came and listened. The speech bubble out of the canary's mouth says, "Oh my!"
7. The dragon received the gold watch and chain from the treasure.
8. During the celebration, Elmer played his harmonica.

This organizer has much more detail and textual support from the story.

I Know; Now You Know

This is an activity that works well with any curriculum area and any kind of flexible grouping setting. When instructing the whole class, I tend to write many things on the whiteboard as students learn and process information. When a lesson was over, I used to erase the board. As the saying goes, "out of sight, out of mind." My students had a difficult time conversing about what was just taught.

Now, before the board is erased, I write all the pertinent information on index cards. Students come up one at a time and tell me what information they are going to erase. As they erase it, I write it on an index card. The person who erased the information has to take the index card and read it to the class. That student then gives the eraser to someone else and the process continues until all the information is erased and put onto index cards. We have containers in the room for all of our curriculum areas. My categories are: science, social studies, math, reading, writing, and language arts skills. You may have different categories depending upon your curriculum.

Students play the game I Know; Now You Know. Choose a subject area and take all of the cards out of the container. Lay them on the floor, face up, so all students can see them. Call on a student; for example, Marisol. She picks up a card and explains whatever is written on it. She then calls on another child, Tawanda, who must repeat the information. After Tawanda repeats the information, Marisol will say to her, "I know about _____, now you know about _____."

Tawanda now chooses a card and explains the concept that is on that card. She will call on another child, Dom, to repeat the information. After Dom repeats the information, Tawanda will say to him, "I know about _____, now you know about _____." This process continues until all of the cards have been chosen.

If a child needs to choose a card and there is not a card available that can be discussed, then he/she asks for a lifeline. Lifelines are explained on page 28 and 29.

Ideas, connections, and implementation strategies.

Reproducibles

Good Morning, _____	Hi There, _____
Dear _____	Hello _____
Hi _____	How are you _____?
Great to see you, _____	To _____
Happy Day, _____	Welcome, _____

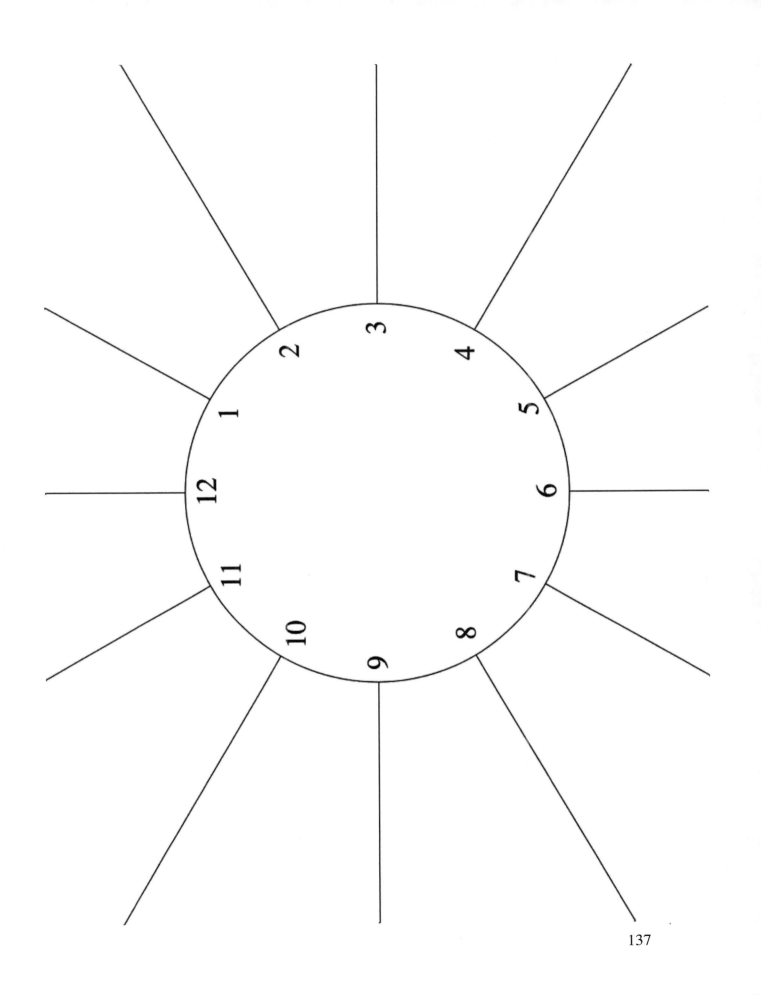

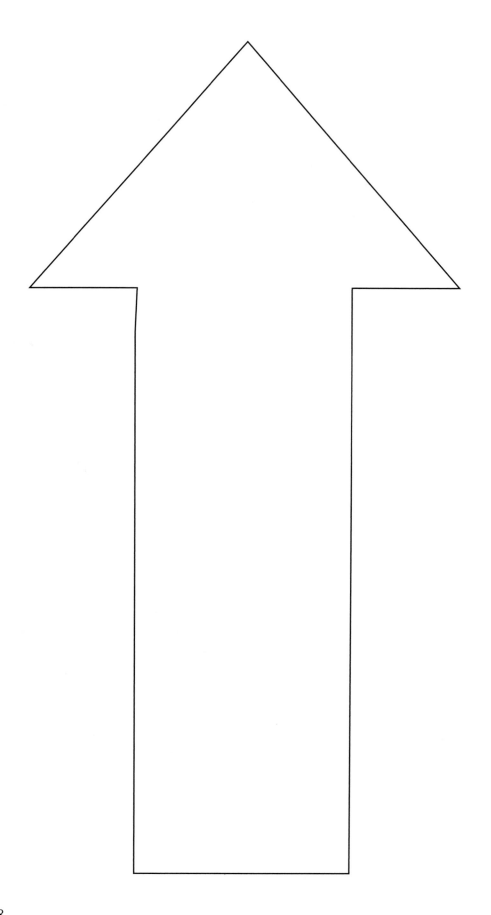

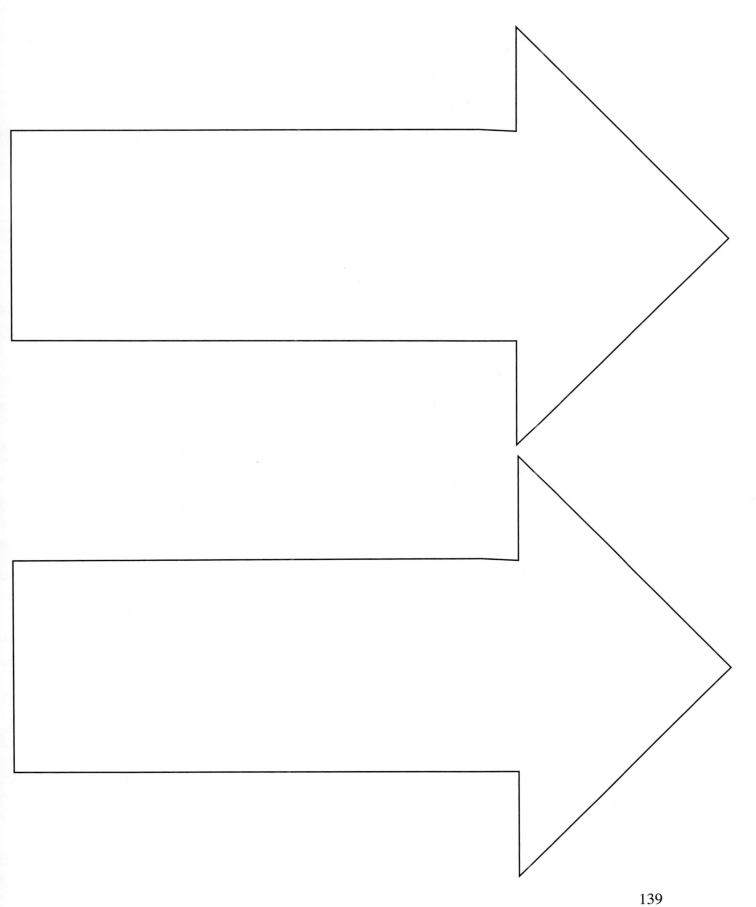

139

```
WHO
is…          did…
was…         can…
will…        wouldn't…
won't…       might…
should…      do you think…
```

```
WHAT
is…          did…
was…         can…
will…        wouldn't…
won't…       might…
should…      do you think…
```

```
WHERE
is…          did…
was…         can…
will…        wouldn't…
won't…       might…
should…      do you think…
```

WHY	
is…	did…
was…	can…
will…	wouldn't…
won't…	might…
should…	do you think…

WHEN	
is…	did…
was…	can…
will…	wouldn't…
won't…	might…
should…	do you think…

HOW	
is…	did…
was…	can…
will…	wouldn't…
won't…	might…
should…	do you think…

"The important thing
is not to stop
questioning!"

Albert Einstein

"The important thing
is not to stop
questioning!"

Albert Einstein

"The important thing
is not to stop
questioning!"

Albert Einstein

"The important thing
is not to stop
questioning!"

Albert Einstein

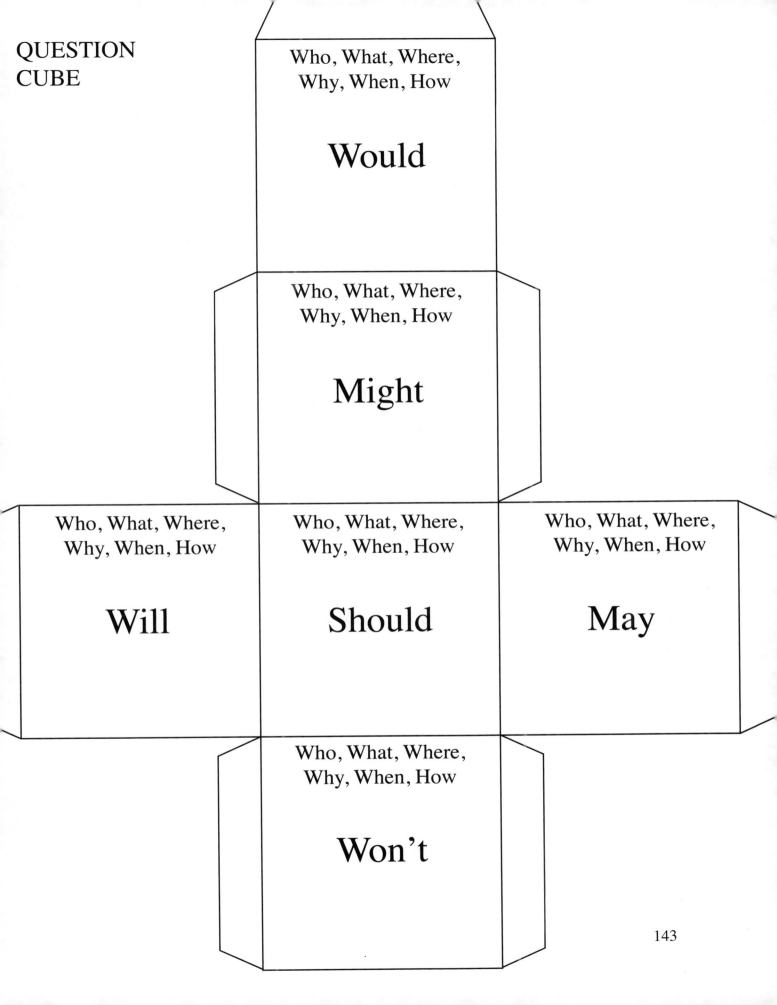

QUESTION CUBE

Who, What, Where, Why, When, How

Would

Who, What, Where, Why, When, How

Might

Who, What, Where, Why, When, How

Will

Who, What, Where, Why, When, How

Should

Who, What, Where, Why, When, How

May

Who, What, Where, Why, When, How

Won't

143

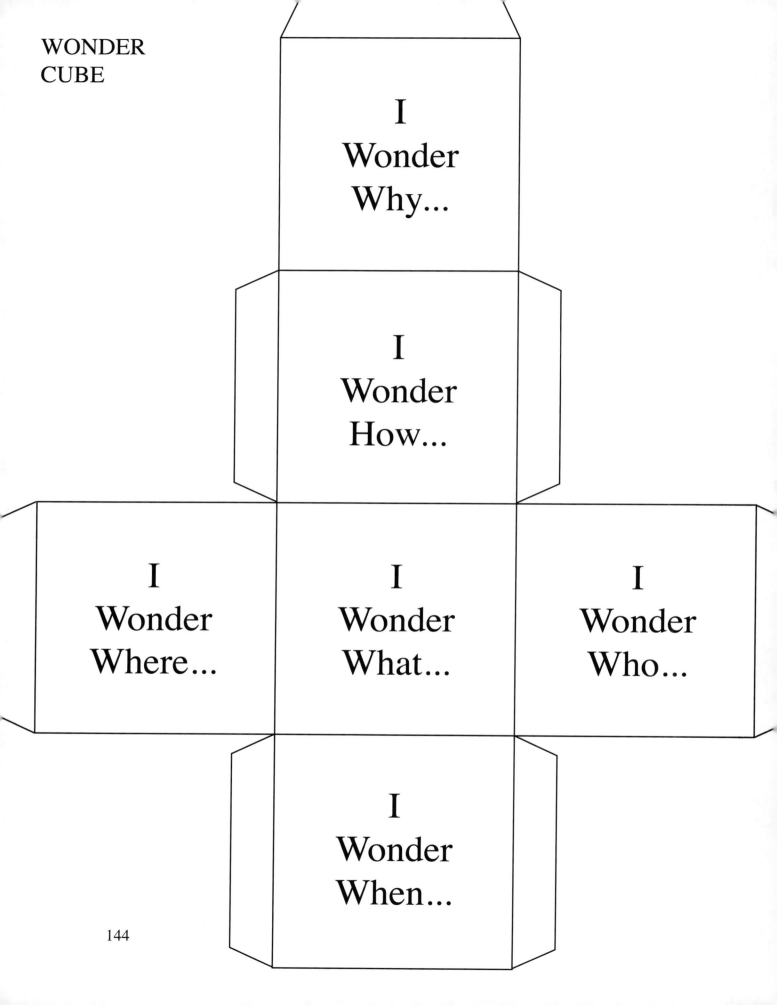

**WONDER
CUBE**

I
Wonder
Why...

I
Wonder
How...

I
Wonder
Where...

I
Wonder
What...

I
Wonder
Who...

I
Wonder
When...

144

STORY
ELEMENT
CUBE

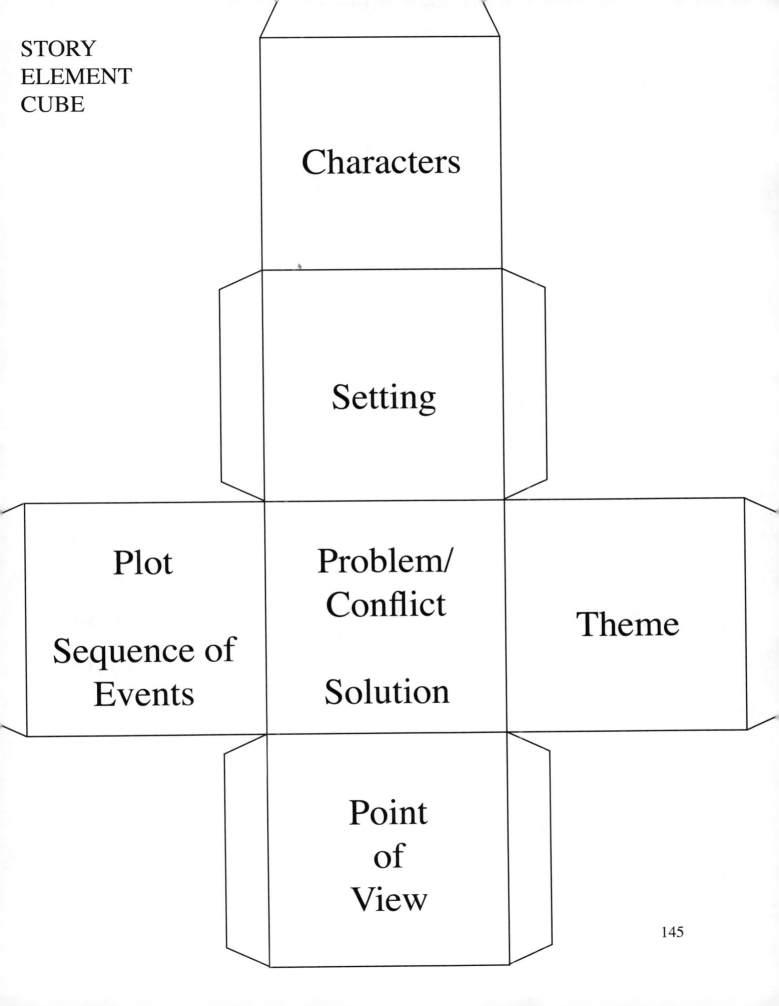

Characters

Setting

Plot

Sequence of
Events

Problem/
Conflict

Solution

Theme

Point
of
View

145

NONFICTION
CUBE

What have you learned?

Look at one of the visuals on the page. What does it tell you?

Compare and contrast 2 things.

Give 5 examples of _____

Explain 2 new vocabulary words from this unit.

Make a connection!

	When I read the part about	It reminds me of
I I		
I I		
I I		
I I		

Text-to-Self	Text-to-Text	Text-to-World

When I read the part about

_____

_____

_____

It reminds me about

_____

_____

_____

- -

When I read the part about

_____

_____

_____

It reminds me about

_____

_____

_____

- -

When I read the part about

_____

_____

_____

It reminds me about

_____

_____

_____

READING
CUBE

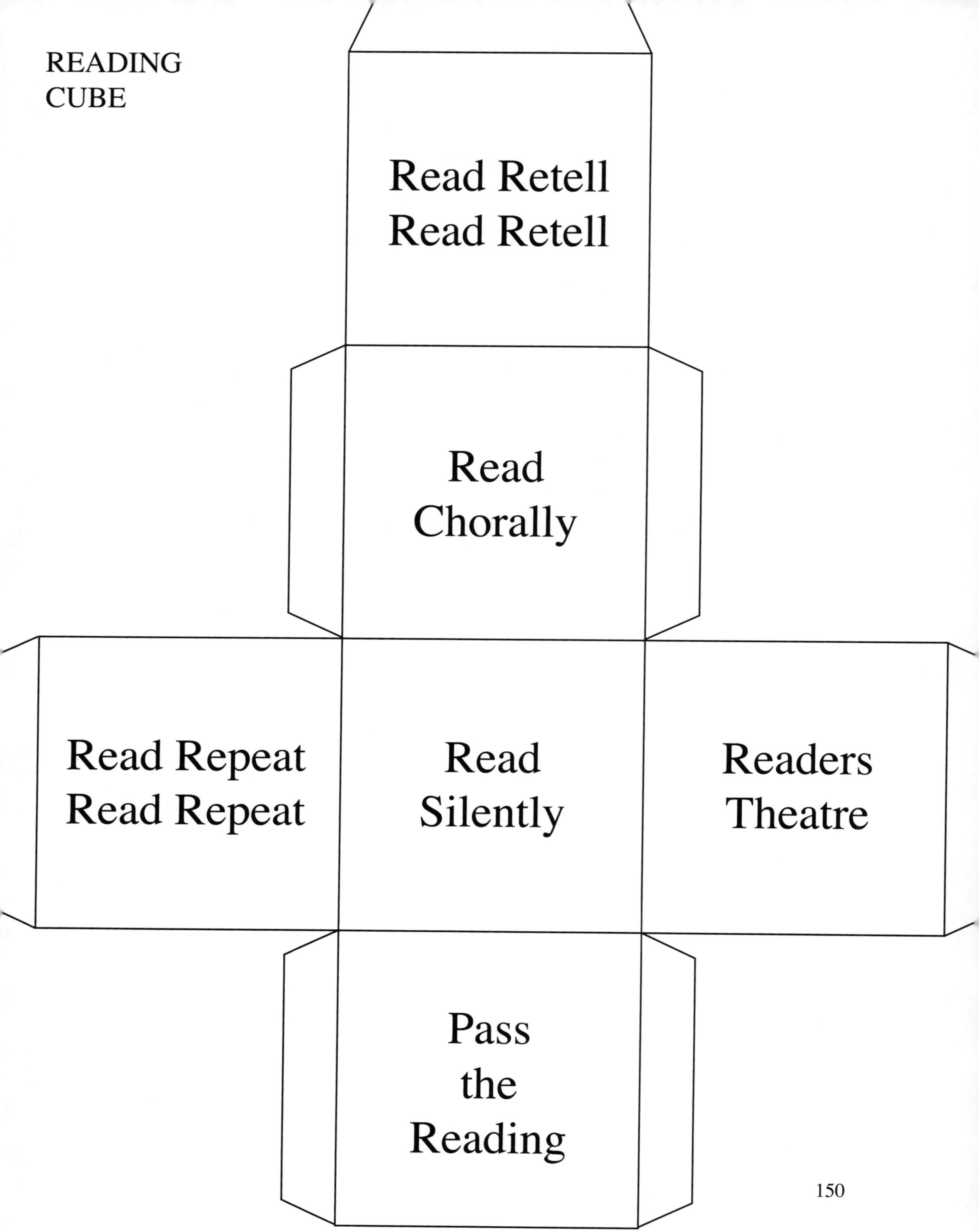

Read Retell
Read Retell

Read
Chorally

Read Repeat
Read Repeat

Read
Silently

Readers
Theatre

Pass
the
Reading

Read Retell Read Retell	Read Repeat Read Repeat
Read Chorally	Readers Theatre
Read Silently	Pass the Reading

Idea shared by

_____

Idea shared by

_____

Idea shared by

_____

Idea shared by

_____

Idea shared by

_____

Idea shared by

_____

Idea shared by

_____

Idea shared by

_____

Idea shared by

_____

Idea shared by

_____

Idea shared by

_____

Idea shared by

_____

Idea shared by

_____

Idea shared by

_____

Idea shared by

_____

Idea shared by

_____

Idea shared by

_____

Idea shared by

_____

Idea shared by

_____

Idea shared by

_____

Idea shared by

_____

Idea shared by

_____

Idea shared by

_____

Idea shared by

_____

Fits Avery Label # 5160

My name is on my paper.

I used 6 colors in my drawing.

I have 10 items/things in my picture.

I have labeled 5 items.

I wrote one sentence.

I wrote three sentences.

I wrote five sentences.

Add a sentence at the beginning of your text.

Add a sentence at the end of your text.

Add 2 sentences in the middle of your text.

Get rid of nice, really, very, said.

Add three words to describe your character.

Describe your setting using the five senses.

Add dialogue in your text.

Have one of your sentences end with an
    exclamation mark.

Fewer Letters Than My Name	The Same Number of Letters as My Name	More Letters Than My Name

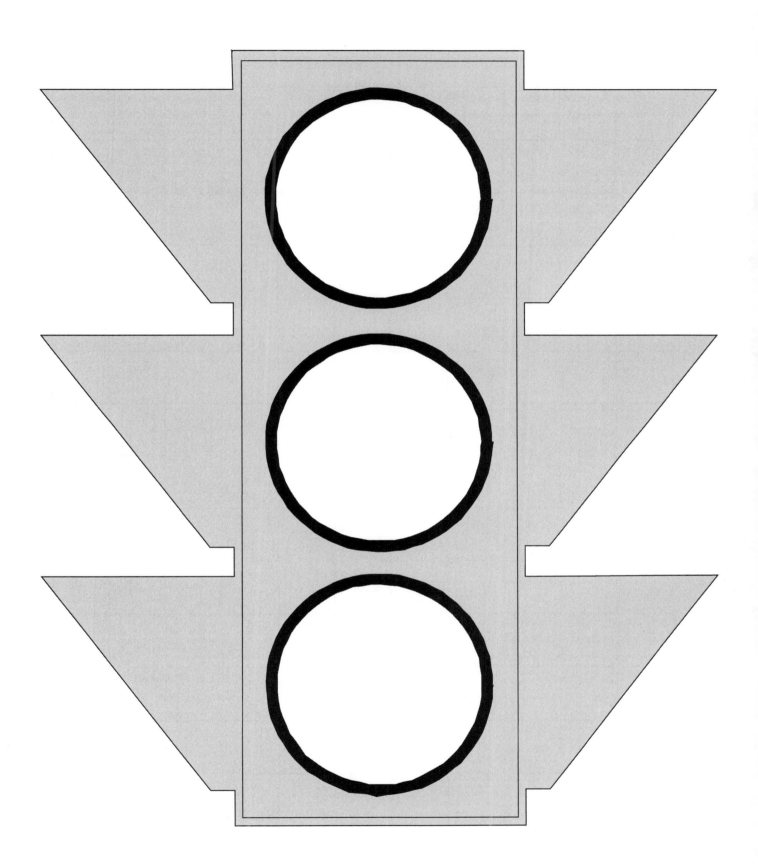

155

Week(s) of _____ _____

Name

Week(s) of _____   _____

Name

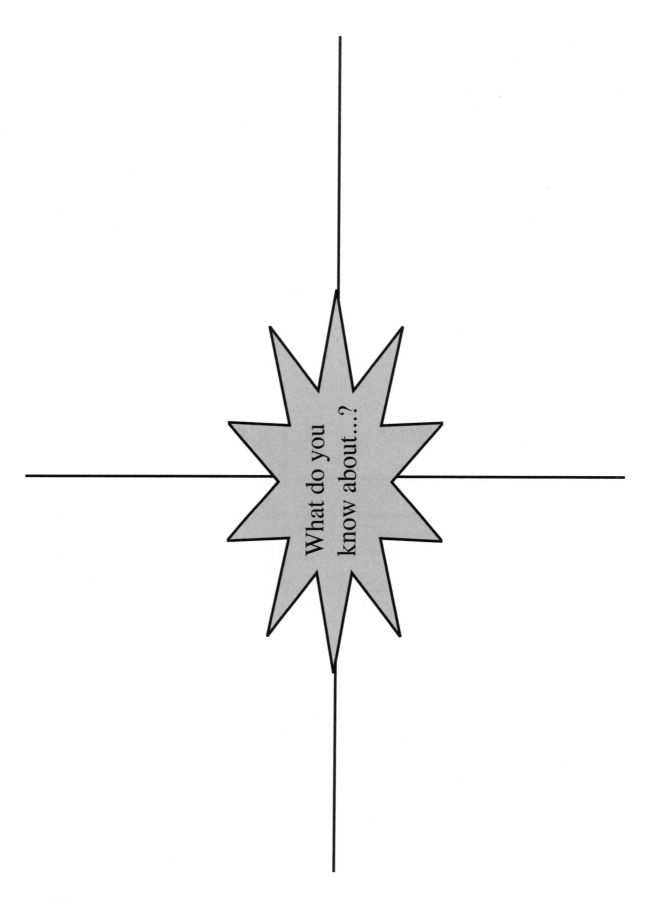

What do you know about....?

ASSESSMENT	CODE
Retelling	BME MEB SL CH S P/S PR

Fluency
 	
    Inattentiveness to punctuation: runs through the punctuation marks.
    Phrasing: student stops at the end of every line at the right side of the page
	//// /—/ —/ — / ———→F
	
	—●—
	
	                               ●
	                               ●
	                               ●

Comprehension	C
Textual support	SUP
Scanning and skimming	SS
Connections	TT TS TW
Vocabulary	Write the word V
Letters	Write the letter
Sight words	Write the word

Running Record
    Omissions
    Substitutions
    Aided Words
    Repetitions
    Self Corrections
    Inattention to punctuation
    Insertions
	
	Circle omission
	Write substitution above word
	P prompt T teacher gave
	Underline
	SC
	Circle punctuation marks
	Draw caret with word

Books Authored by Pat Pavelka

Question Prompts
This is a practical, use it in your classroom tomorrow, guide to help students to independently ask good, thought-provoking questions. This book contains specific prompts for the six question words and nonfiction. Specific ideas and activities for using the prompts are explained. Grades 1-8.

Squiggles
So Much Writing, So Much Fun, So Much Creativity
Helps students develop imaginations, poetry, and stories. Squiggles help differentiate assignments and can be used with students of all ability levels! Grades 1-8.

Cubes
Discussion Activities for Literacy and Skill Development
Teachers will liven up whole group discussions, mini-lessons, and small group inter-actions. Students will apply and utilize skills, not just memorize! Grades 1-8.

Differentiated Assignments
This book demonstrates how to differentiate the daily assignments teachers give students. Teachers plan one activity that can be completed by students of different ability levels. Grades 1-8. Flip tab.

Guided Reading Management
Structure and Organization for the Classroom
This book is a comprehensive manual showing educators how to structure and manage their guided reading programs. Grades 1-3. 158 pages.

Create Independent Learners
Teacher-Tested Strategies for All Ability Levels
This book is full of ideas, strategies, and activities to help all ability-level students become independent learners. Grades 1-5. 160 pages.

Making the Connection
Learning Skills Through Literature
Pat demonstrates how to move toward creating a literature-based reading program that actively involves students in learning. One book is for grades K-2 (136 pages) and one book is for grades 3-6 (144 pages).

Foodle
Foodle is a fascinating fish with an "inter-esting" attribute. Children's book. 32 color pages. Educational activities included.

The Adventures of Victor
Victor the Cat loved his life in the city, but moved to the country. Children's book. 32 color pages. Educational activities included.
CD and Cassette available